ECCLESIASTICAL COURTS, OFFICIALS & RECORDS

SIN, SEX AND PROBATE

Colin R Chapman

SECOND EDITION

LOCHIN PUBLISHING

This is another in the series of Chapmans Records Cameos designed for social, local and family historians world-wide. This Cameo and others in the series by the author originated as his lectures, many of which are profusely illustrated with pertinent examples. The author will, accordingly, be pleased to lecture to family history, genealogical or other societies or groups on the subject of this Cameo or other matters of interest to the social, local and family historian.

The cover illustration is adapted by Nick Ind from a woodcut of an ecclesiastical court from S Bateman's "A Crystall Glasse of Christian Reformation", 1569, showing the ecclesiastical judge as an ass.

Published by
LOCHIN PUBLISHING
6 Holywell Road, Dursley, GL11 5RS, England

First Edition 1992 (1 873686 03 X)
Second Edition 1997
Copyright of the Lochin Publishing Society 1992, 1997

British Library Cataloguing in Publication Data
Chapman, Colin, 1939-
Ecclesiastical Courts, Officials & Records - 2 Rev. ed
(Chapmans Records Cameos Series)
I. Title II. Series
262.9
ISBN 1 873686 15 3

Contents

Preface

"It was on that stone seat that the Church Court used to sit." As a small boy being shown around the church of St John the Baptist at Barnack on the Northamptonshire/Lincolnshire border (since 1974 on the Cambridgeshire/Lincolnshire border), I recall picturing the court officials as garden gnomes, not exactly with fishing rods, but about the same size to be able to squeeze onto the seat a mere four feet long in its triangular-headed recess. I had been taken to Barnack and neighbouring Wittering to compare their Saxon towers with those of Brixworth and Earls Barton, the Northamptonshire homes of dozens of my direct ancestors.

I later learned that this seat in the west wall of the tower, with two others in the side walls, had been discovered during restoration work in 1854, and so the court may not have comprised midgets after all. Unfortunately the two other seats were removed during the alterations, although reference to their use by the president and assistant officers of the local church court was made by the incumbent, Henry F Syers, in a paper he presented to the Architectural and Archaeological Society of Lincolnshire and Nottinghamshire; this was subsequently published in the Journal of Associated Architectural Societies in 1895, on pages 143 to 151.

I was disappointed, therefore, on returning to Barnack in 1991 when preparing the first edition of this Cameo, to discover in its 1968 guide book, re-published in 1990, that this formerly world-famous seat was dismissed with the comment that it "probably had a ceremonial purpose of some kind" - and the other, missing, seats are referred to as aumbries with "no documentary evidence informing us of their use". I cannot believe the nineteenth century antiquaries and ecclesiastical historians got it so wrong; and as a child I certainly marvelled at the endurance, perhaps resilience, of the officials who must have had a most uncomfortable time while the court was in session. At least the seats in my classroom though hard were of wood and not quite as cold in winter as that in the west wall of the tower at Barnack. My sympathy for those ecclesiastical court officials obviously lingered on in my mind, although at that time I had only a vague notion of what went on during a church court hearing.

Also in my dim and distant past I had attended service after service in various parish churches and had been disenchanted by the non-participatory nature of most sermons, that no doubt some clergymen had burned the midnight oil in their preparation. Being an inquisitive child, during many a sermon I browsed through the *Book of Common Prayer*, discovering scores of fascinating facts. Among the passages that caught my eye was the reference to "unquiet disobedient and criminous people" who were likely to be punished by a bishop. I well remember

1

contemplating the congregation and wondering who were the disobedient and criminous ones: possibly the lady behind the pillar under the flower-trimmed hat - all ladies wore hats to church, even to shopping, in those days; or perhaps it was the man across the aisle on crutches with only one leg - artificial limbs were less common than pinned-up trouser legs then - but I remember deciding that he had been punished already by the loss of his leg. I knew that I was one of the unquiet ones - I had often been accused of that - and it was with some trepidation that I anticipated the arrival of the bishop, wondering what punishments we each were going to receive.

I presumed our punishments were not going to be the ceremony of bell, book and candle, for those found guilty of heresy, which accompanied anathematization or excommunication - another scene that had lingered in my youthful mind. The vivid mental picture of a bishop surrounded by twelve priests, all holding lighted candles and dashing them to the ground after the bishop had slammed his book shut while a bell was woefully tolled, was ingrained into my memory many years ago. I do not remember from where this picture came; it cannot have been from the television, for there was none for me to see in my childhood; perhaps there had been an item about it on Children's Hour. I was, and still am, an avid listener to the wireless, from which one can glean far better images than any cinema or television or video can ever provide. Whatever its origins in my mind, the picture of punishment for heresy never left me.

When studying Chaucer at school I had come across the *Friar's Tale* in which part of the work of an archdeacon in the fourteenth century was exemplified. Having to translate the text into the English of the 1950s took away from me some of the enjoyment of the story, but the archdeacon's dealings with witchcraft and fornication appealed to me as a teenager; and although I was less attracted by his involvement in defamation and those who failed to pay the small tithes, I warmed to him as a character with an intriguing job in the local community. Sadly, I was never able to reconcile this image with the archdeacon I had seen - a familiar figure on his bicycle in the community of my youth.

It was when I became immersed in local history research that I began to examine inventories in some depth. This led me naturally to other probate material and then to the workings of the testamentary courts. In studying their documents I found several cases being disputed where I stumbled into the hierarchical structure of the courts' appellate system. It was here I discovered at first hand that some of the church courts dealing with probate appeared to be dealing with all sorts of other interesting business, including the witchcraft and fornication on which the archdeacon of my adolescent reading had pronounced judgment.

Around the time that I was unravelling the organisation of the ecclesiastical courts to my own satisfaction I became involved in family history; I recognised immediately the value of these records in genealogical research. The voluminous records generated at the court sittings, bubbling over with names, ages, addresses and occupations of witnesses, defendants and others had scarcely been touched for centuries, apart from the probate material and marriage licences. And yet these offer such rich sources for studies of migration and British social, and even local, history and provide delightful vignettes of individuals involved in the Church and give details on some school teachers, midwives, surgeons and physicians.

But I was disappointed how little information on the courts and their officials was being promulgated within genealogy and family history groups. In a typical lecture programme the very mention of the words "Ecclesiastical Courts" frightened away many an audience, although everyone was talking about wills. Looking for published material was equally frustrating: a few papers had been presented in the nineteenth century to learned groups and, more recently, specialised analyses of particular courts had been undertaken for very limited years by scholars in the field. There were, of course, the standard works of Swinburne *Briefe Treatise of Testa-ments and Last Willes* (1590), of Conset *The Practice of the Spiritual Courts* (1700), and of Coote *The Practice of the Ecclesiastical Courts* (1843), in addition to the eighteenth and nineteenth century volumes by Burn and Phillimore on *Ecclesiastical Law*; but there appeared to be nothing in an understandable language offering an overview of the ecclesiastical courts, their officials or their records.

In preparing my Cameo on *Marriage Laws, Rites, Records & Customs*, I had dug extensively into Wilkins' *Concilia*, published in 1737. In so doing I had found copious accounts of councils and synods and proclamations of the early Christian Fathers, including Greenfield's 37 *Constitutions* announced in 1311 when he was Archbishop of York; a great deal of the material gathered together by Wilkins is of direct application in the church courts. I later browsed through translations of Lynwood's *Provinciale*. When pulling my disparate notes together for this Cameo I re-read the 1856 edition of the 1832 *Report of the Royal Commission on the Ecclesiastical Courts* and the *Report of the Royal Ecclesiastical Courts Commission* of 1881-1883 with the historical notes by Dr William Stubbs. These fourteenth to nineteenth century works had given me the perfect background for my comprehension of the ecclesiastical courts. I trust that some of that has permeated the following pages to enable you to share that comprehension.

I glimpsed at the situation in Scotland, aware that it was formally within the Province of York until 1192, and that in 1487 the Archbishop of St Andrews became Primate of All Scotland, and thus on a par with the Archbishop of Canterbury as Primate of All England (and Wales), but I decided to exclude Scottish courts from this Cameo.

Nevertheless, I could not have picked my way unaided through the ecclesiastical courts' documentation. I must thank especially the staff of Lambeth Palace Library and the Public Record Office, and those of the Borthwick Institute of Historical Research at the University of York, who have provided the snippets that made the dry legislation spring into life, sometimes joyous, sometimes melancholy, but always vibrant. The staff of the British Library in central London, those in the Embankment Library of King's College, London, and at Bristol University Library have, once again, furnished texts, pamphlets and books for me to study many contemporary works. The county archivists and their staff in Bedford and Northampton have been extremely helpful in providing original documents relating to ecclesiastical courts for my research during the past 30 years.

The First Edition of this Cameo was entitled *Ecclesiastical Courts, Their Officials and Their Records*, and sold thousands of copies, many to present-day ecclesiastical lawyers who thanked me for providing "at long last" an exposition that even they, within the profession, could understand without too much effort. But I was disappointed that so many others, like the family historians I have mentioned above, shied away from the very word "ecclesiastical", so neglecting the possibilities that church court records offer towards their research. As a considerable number of the causes in the ecclesiastical courts dealt with sin, sex and probate, I believe that the baser alternative title will enable this Cameo to get to those parts, perhaps for a crisper read, that the original title failed to reach.

Like my other Cameos, this also had its birth in a number of lectures, on this occasion spanning the variety of activities conducted in the ecclesiastical courts by their officials. I must, therefore, thank Donald Hirst who encouraged me to turn these lectures into a textual format, Keith Pritchard who converted my initial text into a form suitable for the present edition, and Pauline Litton who was an in-defatigable source of assistance in the final stages of its preparation, particularly with details on probate in the Province of York. In revising and re-writing my words, egged on by fellow members of the Selden Society, I was compelled to check the many references I had collected over the years, and I have included many of the relevant Acts of Parliament. Thus those of you who feel so moved will be able to read the detail in those for yourselves. A perusal of even a small proportion of what must amount to several tonnes of documents relating to the ecclesiastical courts and their officials will enable social historians, ecclesiastical historians, genealogists, family historians and biographers all to become intimately involved with the subjects of their research. There is no substitute for turning to original sources, and if this Cameo encourages any of you to do just that, it will not have been published in vain.

COLIN R CHAPMAN.

1. The Ecclesiastical Legal System

Components of Ecclesiastical Law

The Christian Church in Anglo-Saxon Britain was determined to promote faith in Jesus Christ and improve the moral standards of the Angles, the Saxons and the pagan Britons. In its endeavours the Church exercised a strange mixture of customised *Carolingian ecclesiastical law* combined with *secular law* which the bishops (and archbishops) and the temporal judges administered side by side. Ecclesiastical law comprised four essential elements: **civil law, canon law, common law** and **statute law**, though some regard civil law as being part of canon law.

Strictly **civil law** was the old civic law of the Roman Empire which embodied the *Institutes*, *Code* and *Digest* of Emperor Justinian, compiled in the year 533, and incorporated his and his successors' *Novel Constitutions*.

Canon law was (and is) Roman Ecclesiastical Law founded on the civil law but comprising Foreign Canon Law, the Legatine Constitutions and the Provincial Constitutions. The Foreign Canon Law originated from the opinions of the ancient Latin Fathers, the decrees of the General Councils and decretals (letters and Bulls) from various Popes. On its own it was not binding on the English church courts unless any of its elements were specifically sanctioned by English common law; there was, however, often some confusion in the English ecclesiastical courts as to which elements had actually been adopted. Generally it seems to have been accepted that the principles on which Lyndwood had expounded in his *Provinciale seu Constitutiones Angliae* [1.1] in 1432, applied in England and in Wales; William Lyndwood was not only an English bishop but a much respected fifteenth century authority on canon law; the 1679 edition of his work was still being quoted in the twentieth century.

The Legatine Constitutions were those laws which had been passed in national synods or synodals under the chairmanship of the Papal Legates, Cardinals Otho and Ottobon, in the thirteenth century. From around this time the English archbishops arranged for themselves to be appointed as the Pope's legates, and so any additional legatine functions that may have been needed were automatically passed on through the archbishops - until the Reformation when Cranmer had this disavowed in Convocation (see Chapter 4).

The Provincial Constitutions were decrees emanating from provincial synods under the chairmanships of various archbishops of Canterbury from the thirteenth to the early fifteenth centuries; they were adopted in the Province of York in 1462. These were very conveniently transcribed, assembled and published by David Wilkins in 1737 in his *Concilia* [1.2].

On the Reformation Henry VIII forbade further teaching of canon law, but he kept it in place, and left its enactment to the civil lawyers who, naturally, perhaps even subconsciously, influenced it over a period of time. Notwithstanding, Henry directed, by the Submission of the Clergy Act of 1533 [1.3], that the canon law should be reviewed and that until the review was complete those "canons, constitutions, ord-inances, and synodals provincial, being already made which be not contrariant or repugnant to the law of the realm nor to the damage of the King's prerogative, shall still be used and executed". Over the following four centuries, as the review had not been completed, the only authority that canon law had in England and Wales was from the 1533 Act; this really meant that whilst all canons prior to 1533 were binding on both clergy and laity, after that year they applied only to the clergy - unless a layman held an ecclesiastical office.

Henry's Submission of the Clergy Act, with seventeen other of his Acts relating to the Church, was repealed under Philip and Mary in 1554 [1.4], but was revived by Elizabeth I's Act of Supremacy in January 1559 [1.5] and upheld into the present century. At a Convocation on 25 June 1604 the 141 canons of 1603 were enacted, 97 of which were adopted from earlier material; whilst sanctioned by James I, these were never ratified by Parliament. Thus, although they were generally followed, they were not literally binding on the laity and may not have been binding on the clergy either.

Common law was the civic law of the realm of England and Wales, and later also Scotland. **Statute law** was composed of all laws passed by Parliament and published as its Acts. After King Henry's 1533 Submission of the Clergy Act [1.6] most ecclesiastical legislation was incorporated explicitly or implicitly into statutes. For example, the use of the *Book of Common Prayer* was embodied in the 1662 Act of Uniformity [1.7], while the *Thirty Nine Articles* were within the legislation of 1571 [1.8] and 1865 [1.9].

In those cases where there was conflict between the above four elements of ecclesiastical law, civil law submitted to canon law, both to common law and all three to statute law [1.10].

Episcopal responsibilities
In the early mediaeval period of British history a bishop was expected to champion the improvement of the moral fibre of those in his care. A system of, originally annual, *Visitations* was devised to enable him to exercise Quality Management Control over his flock, as quite naturally he was regarded and acted not only as a spiritual leader and benevolent pastor but also as an arbitrator for, and judge of,

those clergy of his flock who failed in their responsibilities. Anciently a Visitation of a parish was termed a Parochial Visitation while a view of a diocese or a diocesan district was termed a General Visitation - so grand an affair that even in 1200 the Council of London accepted a decree of the third Lateran Council (1197), restricting an Archbishop's retinue on a Visitation to 40 or 50 men and horses. This system, somewhat modified to reduce the excessive expenses of a General Visitation, continued after the Reformation, the new procedures being promulgated in 1603 through Canons CIX and CXIX (109 and 119). The Visitation could be conducted by the bishop himself or by Commissioners acting on his behalf; comparable Visitations were conducted by an archbishop or his representative (normally every three or four years, or when a new archbishop was appointed) or by an archdeacon (in some circumstances every three or four weeks) in their own areas of responsibility.

The term Visitation is somewhat misleading: in some cases a bishop toured his diocese to meet church officials to discuss various aspects of Christian faith and conduct what amounted to a Visitation Court hearing; in other cases the Visitation was conducted by officials visiting the bishop at his diocesan headquarters or at other chosen locations in the diocese. In most instances the bishop sent out *Articles of Enquiry* or *Articles of Visitation and Enquiry* (a series of written or printed questions) prior to the Visitation with a schedule of interview dates and locations. An example of 47 questions asked by the Archbishop of Canterbury in 1741 under eight headings is quoted verbatim in Chapter 2. Examples of some late nineteenth century Articles of Enquiry and responses were published by the Northamptonshire Record Society in 1992 [1.11]. The names on the Visitation mailing list (those clergy and others, originally questmen, but later churchwardens and schoolteachers, summoned to attend), were entered into a *liber cleri* (a *call* or *exhibit book*) under their rural deaneries. Following a Visitation, the *detecta* (replies) from the parish churchwardens formed the basis for their *presentments*, by which they presented causes at, for example, a correctional court. These would be regarded as Office Cases following either Plenary or Summary procedures, fully described in Chapter 8.

A bishop additionally passed judgment on laity as well as on clergy who broke the Christian laws of faith and conduct; hence unacceptable responses to an Enquiry could result in an ecclesiastical reprimand, possibly at a Correction Court. A bishop was, in effect, a sort of spiritual lord of the manor, graciously exercising a fatherly control and giving permission to clergy and laity alike to go about their activities; on occasions a fee was extracted, in return for which the bishop granted a dispensation (see Chapter 3) or licence for them to continue in their work. It was equally accepted that those who failed to pay or procure the requisite permission, or who were deemed incompetent in their duties, could be brought before the bishop or his representative at an appropriate Church Court to account for their behaviour.

Origins of the courts

Over the years a variety of ecclesiastical courts grew up to deal with the large number of ecclesiastical causes. Subsequent chapters of this Cameo, 3 and 4 in particular, describe some of these courts which developed from those of the bishops and archbishops. It has been estimated that in the five hundred years between 1300 and 1800 up to nine million cases, involving about ten per cent of the adult population, were heard in the ecclesiastical courts - and half of these were between 1450 and 1640. Deponents alone in the cases made up about seven per cent of the adults. The bishop and his colleagues constantly referred to the Pandora's Box of ecclesiastical laws when making a decision on how to deal with each case they were asked to consider: whether to issue a licence, or grant a faculty, or impose a sentence or punishment on an accused who was found guilty. Considerable guidance through terms of reference for the ecclesiastical courts was provided by the Canons referred to above: Canons 92 to 108 were especially applicable to those courts which came under the jurisdiction of an archbishop, while Canons 109 to 126 were directed towards the courts of bishops and archdeacons and the proceedings which should have taken place in them.

The decisions, many of which involved sentences (see Chapter 9), were imposed at a formally convened ecclesiastical or church court normally held in the church building, often in a specifically allocated space. In the eighth century, for example, Archbishop Cuthbert added an annexe to Canterbury Cathedral to accommodate the court, a baptistery and a mausoleum. In the eleventh century at Barnack in Cambridgeshire stone seats, as discussed in the Preface, were installed in the walls of the ground floor of the tower for those presiding over the court hearings. Archdeacons' courts (see Chapter 3) were often held in a parish church, at the western end of an aisle and, as mentioned above, as frequently as once a month in some parts of the country to enable them to cope with all their correctional and other business.

Secular influence

But it was not only the Christian Church that was interested in the morals of the nation; the Crown was also concerned for national morals, but it went out of its way to ensure that the Church took care of certain aspects of individual and community life. A mere six years after his invasion of England, the Norman Conqueror, William I, issued an Edict in 1072 by which the ecclesiastical courts were separated from the temporal common law courts. The judicial functions of the ecclesiastical courts were confirmed and the presiding officials were extended from archbishops and bishops to include archdeacons. In fact, it is likely that the archdeacons' courts were especially created to cope with the Conqueror's new Edict, which specified that "no bishop or archdeacon shall henceforth hold pleas involving ecclesiastical law in the hundred courts, nor bring to judgment of laymen causes that pertain to the cure of souls; but whoever, according to ecclesiastical law, is summoned for any cause or offence shall come to the place chosen or named by the bishop and shall there respond to the accusation, submitting to the justice of God and of his bishop, not according to judgment of the hundred, but according to the canons and ecclesiastical law".

Accordingly no sheriff, reeve, baron or other layman could henceforth interfere in the workings of ecclesiastical courts. This proved reasonably successful from 1072 to the present - except during the Civil War and Interregnum period - with the result that the ecclesiastical courts have existed and functioned alongside the temporal courts, though with their power gradually decreasing from around the time of the Restoration of the Monarchy in the seventeenth century. Whilst the Edict instigated separate courts it did not instigate the judicial roles which were undertaken in these courts; the roles themselves had belonged to the Apostles. For example, Peter [1.12] had adjudicated in the case of Ananias and Sapphira, and Paul [1.13] had condemned members of the Corinthian Church for breaking the Church's moral laws. It was a fundamental belief of the early Church, perpetuated in the British Public Schools system [1.14] and the British Army, that maintenance of discipline created better disciples. Notwithstanding the fact that the Crown enouraged the Church to become involved in secular matters, it was significant that William I and successive monarchs discouraged the Popes themselves from interfering too much in England.

Whilst the 1072 Edict required, for example, matrimonial disputes to be dealt with in the ecclesiastical courts, disputes over property that a wife brought to a marriage, and any debts incurred by her, were handled at Common Law in the civil courts. The civil courts also heard some cases of injured feelings, although defamation (see Chapter 2) was dealt with in the church courts. Equity Law also was invoked for alimony disputes and for marriages of wards of chancery, such as orphans and lunatics, in which case the Chancery Courts became involved. For further details on these issues see the Cameo *Marriage Laws, Rites, Records and Customs* [1.15]. It should not be overlooked that notwithstanding the above, William I and successive monarchs always managed to keep the Popes out of English government.

Other influences

Some theses on developments of the ecclesiastical courts refer to a major upheaval at the Reformation. These proposals are largely misplaced: whilst there were changes in doctrine and liturgy and an increasing influence of civil law, the organisational structure of the Church, and particularly the church courts, remained mostly intact - apart from modifications demanded by the elimination of Papal jurisdiction and its replacement by Royal supremacy. Of far greater significance was the reorganisation in the nineteenth century when enormous chunks of the responsibilities and work of the church courts were placed in secular hands.

An irritating hiatus in the seventeenth century was the disruption of the ecclesiastical courts in England and Wales during the Interregnum. The granting of probate, for example, was initially restricted to be only in the Prerogative Court of Canterbury but from 1653 [1.16] even that court was closed and probate was granted by civil judges for the "Proving of Wills and Craving of Letters of Administration". (Some manorial courts traditionally had the right to grant probate and a few of these continued to operate during this period.) The church courts were re-opened at the Restoration of the Monarchy in 1660. Although the situation in Scotland is not being considered in this Cameo, it may be noted that the church courts there did not close during this period.

Twentieth century influences

In the twentieth century, canon law was examined more closely than at any other period in history. Following some resolutions which began in Convocation in 1937 (see Chapter 4), the Archbishops of Canterbury and York set up a Commission which published its report in 1947; this put forward proposals for a revised body of Canons, of which CXII to CXXV (112-125) referred to ecclesiastical courts. This led to the setting up by the Archbishops in 1951 of a Commission on Ecclesiastical Courts which published some *Principles of Reconstruction* in 1954 [1.17], incorporating the draft Canons from the 1947 report. It was suggested that if the proposals of the Commission were accepted "the more efficient and logical functioning of the Church's own legal system may well have a marked effect on its life and witness".

In parallel with the above in 1954 there was the publication of *The Revised Canons of the Church of England Further Considered*, in which all the Canons were reproduced in their redrafted form. This promoted further debate and by November 1959 each Canon had been further reviewed, some Canons were redrafted and renumbered, others eliminated and some new ones propounded. These proposals were published in 1960 as *Canon Law Revision 1959*. The discussions continued with further Canons being proposed in 1964 and further revision in 1969; this culminated in *The Canons of the Church of England* being published in 1969. The reorganised and renumbered Canons proposed in 1959 were adopted in principle and the Canons of 1603 effectively supplanted - apart from some detail which is beyond the scope of this Cameo. In general, apart from a note on the Representative Church Council, the Church Assembly and the General Synod on page 78, the remainder of this Cameo addresses the ecclesiastical legal system and the ecclesiastical courts prior to the mid-twentieth century changes identified in this paragraph.

2. Causes in the Courts

Nature of the causes

The situation when an individual was seen by a bishop, or any matter presented, or brought, before an archbishop, bishop, archdeacon or other ecclesiastical judge at a Church Court was known as a *cause*. For example, from the thirteenth century the ecclesiastical courts made decisions on the competence of a clerk being presented to a bishop for institution to a benefice. A court had no hesitation in commenting on a clergyman's faith, his practice, his dress and his behaviour both in and out of church. The courts were further concerned with what were normally non-controversial matters, such as granting probate or ratifying proposed alterations to a church building; some of these causes merely sought approval for specific activities while others involved payment of a tax, a duty or a fine.

These days we would consider that the Ecclesiastical Courts dealt with **sin** whilst the civil courts, including quarter sessions, dealt with **crime**. In the past, however, many offences against God and religion were regarded as ecclesiastical, some even civil, crimes. In the established form for the Consecration of a Bishop in the *Book of Common Prayer* the bishop, as mentioned in the Preface, promises to correct and punish all who "be unquiet, disobedient and criminous" within his diocese.

As intimated in Chapter 1, the ecclesiastical courts offered a correctional forum in which a bishop was able to fulfil his promise by acting as judge over the clergy and laity, particularly if they showed any signs of spiritual back-sliding. Hence most of the ecclesiastical causes were those technically known as criminal suits or "causes for the reformation and correction of manners"; in other words, causes which aimed at correcting (reforming and chastising) those clergy and laity who had contravened the moral code of the Church and so had broken its law of faith and worship - if, for example, a clergyman had not undertaken the duties of his order or benefice. The ecclesiastical courts still remain significant media to deal with such causes, although a bishop's authority over the daily lives of everybody living in his diocese is rarely exercised today; there are many other authorities nowadays who have an obligation to proffer moral advice to their neighbours.

Articles of Enquiry

Many causes were prompted by responses to the *Articles of Enquiry* sent out by an archbishop, bishop or archdeacon prior to a Visitation, mentioned in Chapter 1. The questions followed a similar pattern throughout the country and over several centuries. Those addressed by John Potter, Archbishop of Canterbury in 1741, to the

"Ministers, Church-Wardens and Sidesmen of every parish within the Diocese of Canterbury", were among the most comprehensive [2.1]:

I. Concerning Churches and Chapels; the Fabrick, Furniture, and Ornaments thereto belonging.

1. Have you in your Church, or Chapel, a Bible of the largest Volume, and of the last Translation, together with a *Common Prayer-Book* of the same? Have you the Books of *Homilies* set forth by Authority? A Book of Canons and Constitutions Ecclesiastical; with the printed Table of the Degrees wherein Marriage is prohibited?

2. Is there in your Church, or Chapel, a Font of Stone set in the ancient usual Place, for the Administration of Baptism? Is there a convenient and decent Table for the Celebration of the Holy Communion? Is it covered in Time of Divine Service with a Carpet of Silk, or other decent Stuff, and with a fair Linen Cloth at the Time of the Ministration of the Holy Sacrament? Have you a fair Communion Cup, or Chalice, with Paten and Flagons proper for that Service? Are they kept only for this Use, and not employ'd to any other?

3. Have you in your said Church, or Chapel, a convenient Seat or Pew, for the Minister to read Divine Service in, together with a comely and decent Pulpit for the Preaching of God's Word? Have you a large and fitting Surplice and Hood for the Minister to wear when he officiates in the Church, and especially when he administers the Holy Communion? And is the same Surplice duly washed and repaired at the Charge of the Parish?

4. Is your Parish Church, or Chapel, (as well the Chancel as the Body thereof) in good and sufficient Repair? Are the Roofs thereof well-covered with Lead, Tile, Slate, or other proper Covering? Are the Windows well-glaz'd? Are the floors kept pav'd, plain and even? Are the Seats well and conveniently placed? And are all Things in general, so decently ordered and kept, as becometh the House of God?

5. Have you a Chest for Alms, set and fasten'd in some convenient Place of your Church or Chapel for that purpose, with three Locks and Keys?

6. Have you a Register Book of Parchment, wherein to write the Day and Year of every Christening, Wedding and Burial within your Parish? Are the Names of all Persons Christened, together with the Names, or Sirnames, of their Parents; and also the Names of all Persons Married and Buried in the Parish the Week before, with the Day and Year of every such Christening, Marriage, and Burial, duly enter'd into the said Book, by the Minister of your Parish, in Presence of the Church-wardens? And for the safe keeping of the said Book, have you a Coffer with three Locks and Keys, provided according to the Canon in that Behalf? And is it duly kept there?

7. Have you a Bier, with a black Hearse-Cloth, for the Burial of your Dead?

II. Concerning the Church-yard, the Houses, Glebe, Tythes, and other Dues belonging to the Church.

8. Is your Church-yard sufficiently fenced with Walls, Pales, or Rails? Is it kept decently from all Annoyances? Do you know any Person who hath incroached upon the same, or made

any Door into it out of his own Ground, without Allowance from the Ordinary? Have any Trees growing therein been cut down, and by whom, and for what Use?

9. Is the House belonging to your Minister, together with all the Out-houses thereunto appertaining, kept in good and sufficient Repair?

10. Have any of the ancient Glebe-Lands belonging to your Parsonage, or Vicarage, or any Houses or Out-houses been taken away, or exchang'd, without License of the Ordinary, and free Consent of the Incumbent?

11. Have you a true Terrier of all the Glebe-Lands, Meadows, Gardens, Orchards, Tenements, or Cottages belonging to your Parsonage, or Vicarage? As also a Note of such Pensions, Rate-Tythes, and Portions of Tythes, or other yearly Profits, (either within or without your Parish) as belong thereto? And is your Terrier laid up in the Bishop's Registry?

III. Concerning Ministers, Preachers, and Lecturers.

12. Have you a Parson, Vicar or Curate, legally settled in your Parish? How doth he hold his Living? By Institution and Induction? or by Sequestration? If by Institution and Induction, did he read the Morning and Evening Prayers openly in the Church upon some Lord's day within two Months after his Induction; and declare his unfeign'd Assent and Consent to the Use thereof, as the Act of Uniformity requires? Did he also publickly read the 39 Articles within due time, and declare also his Consent to them in such sort as the Statute in that Case doth direct?

13. Is he defamed, or suspected to have obtain'd his Orders or Benefice by any Simoniacal Compact?

14. Hath he any other Benefice with Cure of Souls? Doth he personally reside upon his Cure in his Parsonage or Vicarage-House? If not, what Curate hath he? And doth that Curate reside among you? What Stipend has he? Does he serve any other Cure besides? What is that Cure? And at what Distance from your Parish?

15. Does he distinctly and reverently read Divine Service at the Time appointed, more particularly on *Wednesdays, Fridays, Sundays* and *Holidays*? And when he reads it, doth he read it audibly and entirely, according to the Form establish'd in the *Book* of *Common Prayer*, without either diminishing in regard to Preaching, or adding any thing not prescribed in the *Book* of *Common-Prayer*?

16. Does he duly bid and observe the Festivals and Fasts of the Church; and use the particular Forms of Prayer appointed for that Purpose? Does he four times in the Year, immediately after Morning Prayers, publickly read the Act against *Profane Swearing and Cursing*? Does he take care to Administer the Sacrament of the Lord's Supper so often, and at such Times that every Parishioner may receive it at least three Times every Year, whereof *Easter* to be one? Doth he, some convenient Time before every Sacrament, give Notice of it in the Church, and read one of the Exhortations appointed for that Purpose?

17. Does he, in the Administration of the Holy Sacraments, in the Celebration of Marriages, in the Office of Churching of Women, visiting the Sick, and Burial of the Dead, follow the Form and Prescription of the same *Book* of *Common-Prayer*; and use all such Rites and Ceremonies in all the other Parts of Divine Service, as are appointed by the said Book?

18.   Does your Minister, when he says the Publick Prayers, or administers the Sacraments, or the other Rites of the Church, wear the Surplice?

19.   Does he (being a licensed Preacher) preach constantly in your Church or Chapel, one Sermon every *Sunday*, unless hinder'd by Sickness, necessary Absence, or some other lawful Impediment?

20.   Doth any Person preach as a Lecturer in your Church or Chapel? Was he, before he entered upon his Lecture, approv'd and licens'd according *to the last Act of Uniformity?* Doth he before his Lecture read Divine Service once every Month, and declare his Assent to the *Book* of *Common-Prayer*, as the said Act requires? And is he in all Respects conformable to the Laws and Orders of the Church of *England?*

21.   Doth your Minister, when he preacheth, use the Form of Prayer before his Sermon which the Canon prescribeth, or some other to the same Purpose? Does he therein pray for the King and Royal Family by Name, as he is ordered and required to do?

22.   Is your Minister ready to baptize your Children in Danger of Death? Have the Children been baptized by him (or in his Absence by any other lawful Minister) at Home, if they have recovered, been duly brought to Church, that the Congregation may be certified that they were rightly baptized, and those Parts of the Office performed which were before omitted? Is there any Child, or aged Person in your Parish, yet unbaptized thro' your Minister's Default? Doth he baptize any publickly without Godfathers and Godmothers?

23.   Doth he diligently instruct the Youth of your Parish in the Church-Catechism, and use his best Endeavour to fit them for Confirmation? Is he ready to baptise Persons of riper Years when occasion requires?

24.   Hath your Minister presum'd to marry any Person without the banns duly publish'd, or a lawful License first had so to do. Has he marry'd any under Age without the Consent of their Parents or Guardians? Has he married any within the Degrees prohibited by the Table of Marriage? Has he done it in any private House, or at Uncanonical Hours, without a special Dispensation to that Effect first obtain'd from the Archbishop?

25.   Does your Minister, as often as there is Occasion for it, take Care to visit the Sick of his Parish, if the Disease be not known or probably suspected to be infectious?

26.   Is your Minister, Curate, or Lecturer, a Man of a sober, peaceable, and exemplary Life? Is he grave and modest in his Demeanor and Apparel? Doth he familiarly converse with any Persons of ill Fame, or excommunicated? Is he a Haunter of Taverns, Ale-houses, or the like publick Places? Doth he lodge in any such?

IV.   Concerning the Parishioners.

27.   Is there any Person in your Parish, that lieth under a common Fame, or vehement Suspicion of Adultery, Fornication, or other Uncleanness? Have you there any common Drunkards, Swearers, or Blasphemers of God's Name and Word? Have you any who stand Excommunicate, or who countenance and keep Company with such?

28.   Do any of your Parish prophane the Lord's Day, by neglecting God's Worship, or doing their ordinary Work, or using any unlawful Pastimes, or Recreations, or permitting their Children or Servants, to offend in any of the aforementioned Particulars?

29. Have you any Person, who under the Pretence of going to some Meeting, tolerated by Law, wholly neglects all publick Worship of God; and neither come to Church, nor go to any such tolerated Assembly for Divine Service?

30. Do your Parishioners demean themselves reverently in your Church, or Chapel, during the Time of Divine Service, and Preaching the Word of God? Kneeling at the *Prayers*; standing up when the *Creed* and *Gospel* are read; saying audibly with the Minister the *Confession, Lord's Prayer* and *Creed*, and making such other Answers to the publick Prayers as are appointed in the *Book of Common-Prayer*? Do any of them loiter, or walk together in the Church-Yard or Church-Porch during the Time of Divine Service?

31. Have you any Parents or Masters of Families, within your Parish, who professing themselves to be of the Communion of the Church of England, do not cause their Children and Servants to learn the Catechism, and do not send them to the Church at the Times appointed to be instructed and examined therein by the Minister, as by the *Book of Common-Prayer* they are required to do? And being sufficiently instructed, do not take care at a proper Age to bring them to the Bishop to be confirm'd by him, in order to their receiving the Holy Sacrament of the Lord's Supper?

32. Are there any in your Parish, who professing themselves to be of the Communion of the Church of *England*, and being above sixteen Years of Age, and sufficiently instructed in Religion, do not receive the Holy Communion at least three Times in the Year, of which *Easter* to be one? Are there any who refuse to receive Kneeling, or from the Hands of their own Minister, repairing for that Purpose to other Parishes? Or are any Strangers who forsake their own Churches, ordinarily suffered to repair to yours, for the same end?

33. Are there any married Women in your Parish, who, after their Delivery from the Peril of Child-Birth, refuse to return their publick Thanksgiving to God, and to make the accustomed Offerings, according to the Appointment of this Church?

34. Are any Wills or Testaments of Persons deceased, within your Parish, that you know of, yet unprov'd? Or any Goods administred without a due Grant from the Ordinary?

35. Have you any in your Parish, who refuse to pay their Duties to their Minister? Or that refuse to contribute, and pay the Rates assess'd upon them, for the Use and Repair of your Church and Chapel, or the Books, Furniture, or Ornaments thereunto belonging?

V. Concerning Church-wardens and Sidesmen.

36. Are the Church-wardens of your Parish, yearly, and duly chosen?

37. Have the former and last Church-wardens given up their Accounts to the Parish; and deliver'd up to the succeeding Church-wardens, the Monies remaining in their Hands, (if any there be) together with all other Things belonging to your Church, or Chapel?

38. Do the Church-wardens suffer any Misbehaviour or Indecency, to be committed in the Church? Do they take care against every Communion, to provide a sufficient Quantity of Bread and Wine for the Communicants? Do they at any Time dispose of the Money given at the Offertory, without the Concurrence of the Minister? Do they give the same to proper Objects of Charity?

VI.   Concerning Parish Clerks, Sextons, and other Officers belonging to the Church.

39.   Have you a Parish Clerk, aged 20 Years at the least; of a sober Life, and good Repute; and sufficiently qualified to perform the Duty incumbent upon him as such? Doth he diligently attend the Divine Service of the Church? Are his Wages duly paid him?

40.   Doth he, or your Sexton (if there be any such appointed in your Parish) take good Care of your Church or Chapel? Doth he see that the Doors be lock'd and open'd at due Times? Doth he keep it clean from Dust and Cobwebs, and other Annoyances? Doth he ring or toll the Bell, at the accustomed Hours before Divine Service, that the People may be warned to come to Church, and in all other Respects diligently perform the Duty of his Office?

VII.   Concerning Ecclesiastical Officers.

41.   Are there any Ecclesiastical Officers, who exercise any Ecclesiastical Jurisdiction within this Diocese, who demand, take, or extort any extraordinary Fees or Rewards, for any Cause? Have any Abuses or Offences been presented by the Church-wardens, and being so presented by them, have been suppress'd, or left unpunish'd? And by what means have they been so neglected?

42.   Hath your Living, when it has been vacant, been committed to honest and sufficient Persons, who have answer'd truly for the Profits thereof, during the Vacancy? And hath your Parish been provided with an able Minister during such Vacancy?

43.   Hath any Ecclesiastical Officers commuted any Penance of any Delinquent convicted, otherwise than by Law is allow'd? And how hath the Money been disposed of?

VIII.   Concerning Hospitals, Alms-Houses, Schools and School-Masters, Chirurgeons and Midwives.

44.   Is there any Hospital, Alms-House or Free-School, founded in your Parish? Who was the Founder, and is now Patron thereof? What is the Endowment or Yearly Stipend belonging to the Governors, or Masters of the same? Are the Revenues thereof rightly employ'd, according to the Intention of the Founder, and of such Ordinances and Statutes as have been made concerning the same?

45.   Doth any Person keep a Publick, or private School in your Parish, who is not allow'd thereunto by the Archbishop, his Vicar General, or other Officer having Authority in that Behalf? Doth every such Master teach his Scholars the Catechism set forth by Authority? Doth he cause them orderly to repair to their Church or Chapel, at the times required by the Canon, and see that they behave themselves there quietly and reverently during the Time of Divine Service and Sermon?

46.   Have you any Parochial Library? If you have, Is it ordered in such sort as the Statute in that Case doth require?

47.   Doth any Man in your Parish take upon him the Practice of Chirurgery, or any Woman to exercise the Office of a Midwife, without Approbation, and License, from the Ordinary to that Purpose?

Although Archbishop Potter died in 1747, it is not impossible that unsatisfactory responses to questions, such as 6, 17 and 24 above, added support to the Marriage Bill finally introduced into Parliament in Lord Hardwicke's name in 1753. See the Cameo *Marriage Laws, Rites, Records and Customs,* published by Lochin [2.2].

Types of causes

Criminal proceedings were taken in the church courts against the laity for certain offences, though few of the following correctional matters are relevant today:

- ♦ heresy, sorcery, witchcraft and failure to attend divine service (thus violating the Christian Church's law of faith and worship)
- ♦ violating the Christian moral code
- ♦ laying violent hands on a clergyman
- ♦ brawling in consecrated precincts
- ♦ defaming a neighbour
- ♦ perjury.

Because the ecclesiastical courts held the responsibility for dealing with all the above, which amounted very much to preserving the social and moral fabric of the nation, resorting for assistance to these courts was, and is still today, necessary for some of the following:

- ♦ sequestration and recovery of tithes, rates and offerings
- ♦ depriving or ejecting a clergyman
- ♦ proving a will or being granted letters of administration
- ♦ obtaining an annulment of a marriage or a separation (but not a divorce) or a licence to become married
- ♦ arbitrating on legitimacy (but not on dower)
- ♦ being granted a faculty to alter the fabric, furniture or ornaments in a consecrated building
- ♦ gaining a licence or being admitted to hold certain positions of influence over others, such as to become a curate, preacher, churchwarden, parish clerk, schoolmaster, midwife, physician or surgeon.

Heresy was regarded as being so serious, both before and after the Reformation, that normally an archbishop dealt with this cause - but, as described in detail in Chapter 3, it was felt so important to suppress the heretics that on occasions they were brought before almost any court in the first instance. *Witchcraft* was treated as heresy from 1258, with persecutions throughout Christendom taking place in great numbers from 1434, intensified by a Bull of Pope Innocent VIII in 1484 - but see

Chapter 9 concerning English sentences for heretics. Sorcery and witchcraft, as secular crimes in Britain, were abolished in 1736, the last execution for witchcraft having been that of Janet Horne at Dornoch in Scotland in June 1727.

Lapses by the clergy from the standards dictated by the Church in terms of *faith and practice* (pastoral work and worship) and *morality* (behaviour and dress) were brought before the ecclesiastical courts, as would be expected. But in addition the ecclesiastical courts were so keen to uphold the clergy as exemplary that they also dealt with any offences that the clergy committed against the criminal laws of the realm. There was also a practical logic in the Church dabbling in such temporal matters: in the mediaeval Church the clergy were exempt from criminal proceedings in the temporal courts, a practice known as "benefit of clergy". However, from the time of Henry VII there was a reduction in the number of offences from which exemption could be claimed, and in any case benefit of clergy was more or less abolished in 1576 [2.3], although it did remain in a limited form until the Criminal Law Act of 1827 [2.4].

Laying violent hands on a clergyman while taking a service and *brawling in consecrated precincts*, as offences over which the church courts had jurisdiction, were removed by the 1860 Ecclesiastical Courts Jurisdiction Act [2.5] to be offences that could be brought before a Justice of the Peace. The offence was extended by this legislation to include any riotous, violent or indecent behaviour in a place of worship belonging to any religious body - not only the consecrated precincts of the Anglican Church, as before this Act.

The offence of *defaming a neighbour*, defamation (sometimes referred to as diffamation) continued to be heard in the ecclesiastical courts until 1855; as an offence it was abolished totally by the Ecclesiastical Courts Act [2.6] of that year. *Perjury* had remained an ecclesiastical offence until 1823 [2.7].

The method of *recovery of tithes* was changed by the 1836 Tithe Act [2.8] and a Tithe Rent Charge was introduced. This could be recovered by distress if necessary from those who were reluctant or who refused to pay the cash; or, if even that failed, by obtaining a writ of possession in the temporal courts. On the other hand the compulsory collection of *Church Rates* continued until 1868 when they were abolished altogether by the Compulsory Church Rate Abolition Act [2.9].

The opportunity to challenge the *competence of a clergyman* to undertake his duties was encompassed in 1840 within the Church Discipline Act [2.10] which laid down very precisely how criminal suits or proceedings should in future be instituted against a priest or deacon, normally in the first instance in the bishop's Consistory Court. The 1840 Act did not, however, revoke the 1838 Pluralities Act [2.11] which enabled clergy to be brought before the Consistory Court if they were non-resident for too long without a licence, or if they were farming more acres than permitted. The 1840 Act confirmed that the *Court of the Archbishop for the Trial of Heresy* and the *Court of the Archbishop for the Trial of Bishops* (see Chapter 4) could be convened if required. An additional court was set up under the 1898 Benefices Act [2.12] to hear cases against a bishop who refused, on grounds other than of doctrine or ritual, to institute a presentee to a benefice. In what really amounted to yet another new court, the Bishops' (Retirement) Measure of 1951 enabled the Church to discipline bishops guilty of unbecoming behaviour, under very specific circumstances. Until then bishops, for many years unlike priests and deacons, had fallen outside the remaining courts' jurisdiction as a result of the closure of many of the ecclesiastical courts.

All *probate* matters and *matrimonial causes*, including validity and legitimacy disputes, could be brought only before the ecclesiastical courts until 1858, as described in some detail in Chapters 3 and 7. The granting of marriage licences remained an ecclesiastical prerogative until 1837, when a Superintendent Registrar could issue a Registrar's Certificate, the equivalent of a Common Licence. Since 1971 the Registrar General has been enabled to issue Registrar General's Certificates, similar to the Archbishop of Canterbury's Special Licences, as described in the Cameo, *Marriage Laws, Rites, Records & Customs*.

It is still necessary to obtain a faculty from the diocesan authorities to change, add to, or remove items from, consecrated premises, and it is still stipulated that certain parochial positions are held only by licensed or approved persons. However, the diocesan licensing of a schoolmaster, midwife, physician or surgeon, introduced by Henry VIII in 1511 [2.13] (to ensure that Popish beliefs are not promulgated in schools, that a reliable Christian woman is at hand to baptise newly-born babies whose lives are at risk, and that magical and sorcerous practices are not being exercised), is no longer required. Incidentally, one of the "conditions" of a mid-wife's licence was for her to discover, from an unmarried mother, the name of her child's father - if necessary refraining from assisting with the delivery until the mother had identified him.

A graphic picture of the causes which an archdeacon encountered in a typical sitting of his court in the fourteenth century can be found in Geoffrey Chaucer's *Friar's Tale*, written about 1390:

> In my district once there used to be,
> A fine Archdeacon, one of high degree,
> Who bravely passed the judgment due
> On fornication and on witchcraft too,
> Bawdry, adultery and defamation,
> Breaches of wills and contracts, spoilation

> Of Church endowment, failure in Church rents
> And tithes, and disregard of sacraments,
> Of simony and usury. But he would boast
> That lechery was what he punished most.
> If any person would to him complain,
> They would escape not from financial pay'ng.
> For small tithes and small offering
> He made the people piteously to sing.
> And ere the bishop caught them with his crook,
> Down they went in the Archdeacon's book;
> For he had, through his jurisdiction,
> Power to give to them correction.

A few causes in the ecclesiastical courts even reached the dizzy heights of *causes célèbres*; although these law suits, which excited considerable public interest, were normally enacted in the common law courts.

Court fees

The fees laid down in 1529 by Henry VIII's legislation for non-judicial business, described in later chapters, were 6s. 8d. (a half-Mark) for faculties for pews (identical to the Doctors' Commons annual subscription - see the commentary in Chapter 7), 10s. for a marriage licence, 5s. for licences for preachers and surgeons, and 2s. 6d. for licences for curates, schoolmasters and midwives. The fee for granting probate and issuing Letters of Administration (admons) depended on the value of the estate: if under £5, for probate and admons the judge received nothing, whereas the registrar received 6d. for probate but nothing for admons; with estates from £5 to £40, for probate and admons the judge received 2s. 6d., whereas the registrar received 1s. for probate and 2s. 6d. for admons; with estates valued over £40, for probate the judge and the registrar each received 2s. 6d. although the registrar could charge 1d. per ten lines of a will, whereas for admons the fees were negotiable. Over the years these fees were modified. Probate accounts, including executors' and administrators' accounts, particularly from the late sixteenth to the mid-eighteenth centuries, in many cases offer details, not available elsewhere, on a testator, or an intestate, and their families and situation at their time of death, as exemplified by Amy Erickson in *The Records of the Nation*, published by the British Record Society in 1988.

3. Ecclesiastical Court Structure

Hierarchical levels

From at least the mid-twelfth century the ecclesiastical courts in England and Wales operated at four levels in increasing seniority from *archidiaconal, diocesan* and *provincial* to *papal*, presided over originally by respectively an archdeacon, bishop, archbishop and the Pope. As the years went by many of the original presiding officers commissioned (delegated their authority to) surrogates to act on their behalf; hence rural deans and chancellors, for example, are found presiding in some courts (see Chapter 5). The advantages of this hierarchical structure were that causes requiring a local input or an immediate response, and of a less serious nature, could be dealt with by the lower courts more easily, more cheaply, and more quickly (as they sat more frequently - in some places every three to four weeks, as mentioned in Chapter 1). Furthermore, if the interested parties were unhappy with the handling of a case, there was a succession of higher courts to which appeals could be made. There were, on the other hand, many causes not of an appellate nature which were dealt with at diocesan and provincial level, for either custom or convenience.

Courts of appeal

Nevertheless, the Court of First Instance was that of the archdeacon and from there appeal was to the bishop's court. From a bishop's court recourse was to the archbishop. Above an archiepiscopal court the appellate court was known as the *Court of Arches* in the southern province and as the *Chancery Court* in the northern province (details on these courts are explained in Chapter 4). The final appeal was, until 1533, to the *Papal Curia* (Papal Court); but, as a result of the Restraint of Appeals Act [3.1] of February 1533, any appeals formerly addressed to the Pope were to be made to the Archbishop of Canterbury, or the Archbishop of York, within fifteen days of the judgment. And then, from Easter 1534, under the Submission of the Clergy and Restraint of Appeals Act [3.2], the final appellate in England and Wales was declared to be to the *Curia Regis* (the King's Court, the Crown in Chancery). The judges were commissioned or appointed "to hear and definitely determine such appeals, and the causes concerning the same". The Crown, removed by William I from the machinations of the ecclesiastical courts, was deliberately brought back to the scene by Henry VIII.

All this was swept aside when Roman Catholicism was reintroduced under Queen Mary in 1553 (see Chapter 1). Then, in 1559, Elizabeth I's Supremacy Act revived some of Henry VIII's Acts, but introduced a *High Court of Delegates* as the appeal court from the Archbishops' Courts. In this Court of Delegates (until 1832), following Henry's model, the judges were appointed specifically for each case by the Lord Chancellor so introducing an element of temporal influence, though not control at this stage, over the spiritual courts. Because the judges were specifically appointed for each case and they never explained the reasons for their judgments (see Chapter 8), no continuity of policy was possible - a major contributing factor in the ultimate demise of this court. An appeal against a decision of this court could be made via a petition to the Crown; and there were many appeals in the early nineteenth century because most of the lawyers in the High Court of Delegates were junior, relatively poorly paid and inexperienced advocates; they were also unwilling to go against any decisions of their more senior colleagues who had already passed judgment in a lower court. Accordingly confidence in the court fell and doubts about the competence of its judges increased. On the other hand their honesty was not in question. If the appeal was successful the case was heard afresh by a Commission of Review presided over by judges who also were appointed by the Lord Chancellor. But this was a lengthy and costly process. A detailed analysis of the High Court of Delegates by G I O Duncan was published in 1971 [3.3].

In 1832, to obviate the above problems and dispel the doubts, the method of appeal from an Archbishop's Court, through the High Court of Delegates to the Crown in Chancery, was dramatically altered by the Privy Council Appeals Act [3.4] to be, from February 1833, direct to the *Crown in Council*; the method of appeal was altered again later in that year [3.5] to be to the *Judicial Committee of the Privy Council*, thus confirming the secularisation of the ultimate appeal that Henry VIII had wrested from the Pope 300 years before. Notwithstanding, the decision in 1833 was not so illogical: by this time the Privy Council was already the supreme court of appeal from the British colonies in ecclesiastical causes.

The composition of the Judicial Committee, which from its inception dealt mostly with matrimonial and probate disputes, indicates its secular nature: the Lord President of the Privy Council, the Lord Chancellor, the Lord Keeper or First Commissioner of the Great Seal, the Chief Justice of the Court of Common Pleas, the Chief Baron of the Court of the Exchequer, the Master of the Rolls, the Vice Chancellor, the Judge of the Prerogative Court of Canterbury (who must have felt extremely vulnerable as the ecclesiastical token in this secular company), the Judge of the High Court of Admiralty (who at this period also had a tenuous connection to the fast-fading ecclesiastical lawyers), and the Chief Judge in Bankruptcy; furthermore the Crown was enabled to appoint two other members to the Committee and direct the attendance of the judges. Further details on the members of this Committee are given in Chapter 10. By 1858 the ecclesiastical courts which had previously dealt with matrimonial and probate causes had effectively been closed as their business had been transferred to the new temporal courts - see below. Thus the final appellate was altered yet again [3.6] and removed from the Judicial Committee of the Privy Council to the *Divorce Court*, for matrimonial causes, and to the *House of Lords*, for probate causes.

Departure from the structure

In practice there were significant deviations in applying the four theoretical levels in ecclesiastical court hierarchy described above. Some reasons for this are explained in paragraphs (a) to (g) which follow.

(a) Certain areas fell totally outside the jurisdiction of an archdeacon or bishop. Some were termed *peculiars*, others *donatives*; these terms are described below.

(b) Several archdeacons' courts had *limited jurisdiction* and so some causes were heard in the first instance in a bishop's court.

(c) In some classes of causes the archdeacons' and the bishops' courts had *concurrent jurisdiction* and so an appeal went from the archdeacon's court direct to the archbishop's court.

(d) During an archbishop's (or bishop's) visitation, which could take many weeks, the lower courts were *inhibited* (closed). All ecclesiastical matters during an inhibition had to be dealt with by a higher court.

(e) The unexpected resignation or death of a court's presiding officer created a *vacancy* which, similarly to an inhibition, caused a court to be temporarily closed; hence its normal business was conducted in a higher court. In many dioceses following the demise of a bishop a successor was often not appointed for several years.

(f) Complicated cases, especially in the twelfth and thirteenth centuries, tended to by-pass all lower courts and were heard in the first instance in the Papal Court, as this was regarded as a Court of First Instance for the See of Rome - in effect for all Christendom - in addition to its role as the senior appeal court. Examples of the complicated cases involved those of a doctrinal or ritual nature, or where the status and influence of the parties were likely to overwhelm a lower ecclesiastical court, or where even a diocesan or archiepiscopal court had no remedy, or if a re-hearing was appropriate. Such cases were not heard actually in Rome, but in England and before bishops who were appointed as papal judges delegate. The Papal Court thus became, in reality, a *Court of Papal Judges Delegate*, though not convened in the normally understood way of a formal court.

In 1971 Professor Jane Sayers published some of the results of her research on the work of the Judges Delegate in the Province of Canterbury in the thirteenth century [3.7]. From the end of that century these cases were heard in the Archbishop's *Court of Audience* (see Chapter 4); from 1533 to 1641 and briefly from 1686 to 1688 this archbishop's court was taken over by the Crown and became the temporal *Court of High Commission*. In the latter year the jurisdiction of the Court of Audience, as described below, was merged with that of the Court of Arches.

(g) Proven cases of heresy in the Canterbury province, according to an ecclesiastical Constitution of 1416, could be dealt with directly by the archbishop in *Convocation* (see Chapter 4), or before an archbishop and a committee of bishops, or before a Commission issued by an archbishop. Punishment for heresy is found in Chapter 9.

Several heresy cases, especially after the Ecclesiastical Jurisdiction Act of 1531 [3.8], were heard in the first instance in an archbishop's court anyway, and some in the sixteenth and seventeenth centuries were even dealt with by the Court of High Commission, as has been debated in some depth by Roland G Usher [3.9]. This temporal court operated in the York province as well as in Canterbury and also in the dioceses (see Chapter 10 for detail on their records). Some High Commission reports which were translated and published in 1886 [3.10] give a marvellous insight to the social and sexual problems of the 1630s; one clergyman was preaching without a licence, another had translated some psalms but then added a scandalous table to them and later wore inappropriate clothes, whilst another (all their names are given) was showing off parts of his anatomy and successfully encouraging various ladies to join him: this cleric was excommunicated, fined £500 and ordered to pay the court costs - not a small sum at that time, or even today.

Usher offers the 1559 Act "for restoring to the Crown the ancient Jurisdiction over the State Ecclesiastical and Spiritual, and abolishing all foreign power repugnant to the same" as an origin for the Court of High Commission. He also refers to the concerted personal attempts by Henry VIII and his children to eradicate heresy. There were, however, earlier Commissions regarding heresy: Wolsey had issued one in 1521 to the bishops to search for heretical books and there had been one to the Bishop of Hereford in 1432 to enquire of persons suspected of heresy [3.11]. Thus a bishop sitting in his palace, or even the Official in a diocesan court, could examine heresy cases. The Crown, over a hundred years before Henry VIII, had been worried about heresy: in 1406 Henry IV issued an emergency ordinance whereby anyone preaching or teaching against the Catholic faith - in other words promulgating heresy - was to be arrested and imprisoned and then taken by the Chancellor to be judged by the King, his heirs and peers of the realm.

Courts' diverse activities

Besides their appellate responsibilities, the diocesan and provincial courts conducted considerable business in their own right. At the diocesan level the courts were variously termed Episcopal, Audience, Consistory or Commissary, by custom or by virtue of the business conducted in them. In the Diocese of London, for example, before the Reformation the Consistory Court was the most senior and followed strict plenary procedures (see Chapter 8) whereas the more junior Commissary Court followed summary procedures. The intricacies of church courts held in London at this time were carefully described by R Wunerli in 1981 [3.12]. The Consistory Court in a large diocese could sit in more than one place, at nominated towns in the diocese, for example, though it was often held in the diocesan cathedral building. On occasions, when the business required delicate handling or if the parties were of prominent social standing, the bishop himself sat as judge. Normally, however, as is dealt with in some depth in Chapter 5, a bishop delegated his duties as judge in the ecclesiastical courts to other officials.

At different periods of time there were often separate courts at both diocesan and provincial levels constituted differently to handle different causes or types of business - Audience Courts and Probate Courts are just two examples. Furthermore, the items of business of these courts frequently ran together and were recorded within the same documentation, perhaps in a bishop's consistory register or in an archbishop's register, and often with poorly defined headings. It is not easy for us, several centuries later, to identify exactly which court was being convened for which causes; if, indeed, it was clear at the time.

In the diocesan audience courts the bishop, or his chancellor, vicar-general or any clerk of the episcopal household specifically deputed by the bishop, heard the cases in the same manner as in an archbishop's audience court (see Chapter 4). The causes that were heard in an audience court dealt generally with the morals of the clergy and persistent lapses of morality by the laity, with important matrimonial cases and with some probate matters. The business in the audience courts of the Lincoln Diocese is among the best documented, and Mrs Dorothy Owen has thoroughly examined some fourteenth century material for Salisbury Diocese (see Chapter 10). The procedures in the probate courts of archdeacons, bishops and archbishops are described in Chapter 8, and in these courts the procedures varied little between the three levels. The higher courts were generally better organised than those beneath them and had better filing systems, and so the families of the clergy and gentry tended to go to those; thus breaking all the rules as to the correct court to attend.

Dispensations, licences etc.

Additionally, the ecclesiastical courts issued *dispensations* (relaxations of canon law) and *licences* for a number of situations. In these situations also, the ecclesiastical court structure required certain hierarchical procedures to be observed, although they were sometimes ignored or circumvented. Prior to the break with Rome, the Pope, and his legates through the Papal Courts, had issued "licences, dispensations, compensations, faculties, grants, receipts, delegacies, instruments and other writings"; but the 1533 Act of Dispensation [3.13] transferred this responsibility to the Archbishop of Canterbury and the Lord Chancellor jointly. They exercised their responsibility through a *Master of the Faculties* from the Faculty Office which was opened in April 1534.

As the See of Rome had done in pre-Reformation times, the Master of the Faculties issued a mass of documents covering a very wide range of activities. Included in the Master's papers were the appointments (throughout the whole of the British Empire in Victorian times) of Notaries Public (see Chapter 6), licences to eat meat in Lent (granted into the seventeenth century), licences to preach, to teach, to practise medicine and surgery and midwifery, the conferring of honorary degrees (see the next paragraph), dispensations for holding benefices in plurality (for a priest to be in charge of more than one parish), or for those who were not in orders to hold a benefice (for persons, though not ordained, to take charge of a parish), dispensations for ordination despite illegitimacy (only legitimate persons could normally become priests), and dismissory letters. Archdeacons' and bishops' courts were also able to issue certain licences.

The accepted practice of conferring degrees, other than by the universities, had been exercised by the Pope through his legates in England and Wales by the fifteenth century; persons so rewarded were known as *Roman Graduates*. The Palatine courts in Durham and Lancaster had also conferred degrees (and incidentally made Notaries by faculty). Some Roman Graduates were later incorporated at British universities though on each occasion this honour was accompanied by the proviso that it should not set a precedent. At the Reformation the term faculties used in the 1533 Act of Henry VIII, referred to above, was interpreted as including degrees; within six years Archbishop Cranmer exercised this right and commissioned the Bishop of Norwich to confer a Doctorate of Divinity on Elgius Ferrers. As the honorary degrees were conferred by the Archbishops of Canterbury from Lambeth Palace they became known as *Lambeth Degrees*. The right was challenged for the first time in 1722 at Lancaster Assizes whence, after a fifteen hour hearing, it was referred to the King's Bench where the challenge was rejected. Besides divinity the disciplines of the degrees were law and medicine - although following the 1858 Medical Act [3.14] degrees in the latter were not accepted as a qualification to practise after 2 August that year.

Probate

With regard to probate, it must be remembered that from the time of the Norman Conquest, or even earlier, England and other parts of the British Isles were administered under a feudal system. Thus on death only personalty (personal estate, the commonly-used term for goods and chattels, is incorrect) was devisable through a testament and the Church assumed responsibility for disposing of the deceased's chattels for the benefit of his soul. Real estate tended to be dealt with by the manorial courts, particularly as the vast majority of land was held by copyhold tenure. Gradually, however, probate included proving wills (devising real estate) as well as testaments and granting *Letters of Administration* if a person died intestate. Normally the probate courts were involved only if the deceased had *bona notabilia* (strictly, an estate worth five pounds or more - but ten pounds in London). Probate and Testamentary Court procedures are detailed in Chapter 8. *Letters of Administration-with-Will-Annexed* were granted when a deceased had failed to name any executors, or the named executors could not (because they were minors, or had died, or could not be found), or would not, execute the will according to the wishes of the deceased. In such a situation administrators were appointed in place of the executors and granted Letters of Administration to administer the attached will.

If the deceased had property in two or more parishes in the same deanery or archdeaconry (unless a peculiar was involved - see below), the will or testament was proved (or letters of administration were granted) in the deanery or archdeacon's court; Canterbury province favoured utilizing archdeaconries, York the deaneries. But if the property was in two deaneries or archdeaconries yet in the same diocese, the bishop's *Consistory* (or *Commissary*) *Court* should have granted probate - but from time to time these "guidelines" were forsaken, particularly by families of the clergy and nobility, possibly because they had a greater insight to the filing systems of the higher courts; if the deceased had property in two dioceses within the same province, the archbishop's testamentary *Prerogative Court* granted probate (but see Chapter 4 for exceptions to this in the Province of York); if the deceased had property in both the Province of Canterbury and the Province of York, the archbishop of the former province claimed superior jurisdiction [3.15] and probate should have been granted in his court; if the deceased had property both within and out of England or Wales (that is in Scotland, Ireland or elsewhere) probate was normally granted in the Archbishop of Canterbury's court. Very occasionally probate was granted in the *Court of Arches*, if a case had been disputed and on appeal had ended up there. The ecclesiastical courts, following the methods described in Chapter 8, continued to grant probate until 1858 when, resulting from legislation of 1857 [3.16], the temporal *Courts of Probate* came into being, as described in Chapter 7, in which temporal lawyers were empowered to act.

Marriage licences

When seeking a common marriage licence almost identical criteria applied as for probate, although an archdeacon could not issue a licence. Thus if both parties came from different parishes which were in the same diocese their bishop (or his representative) granted a *Common* or *Ordinary Licence*; if, however, the parties were from different dioceses but the same province the archbishop did so, and if from different provinces the Master of the Faculties, on behalf of the Archbishop of Canterbury, granted the Common or Ordinary Licence. The Archbishop of Canterbury was also able to issue *Special Marriage Licences*, as is explained in detail in the Chapmans Records Cameo on marriage, referred to above. On the other hand, matrimonial disputes, however occasioned, were dealt with in substantial numbers in the archdeacons' courts and upwards (except when Common or Equity Law was broached - see Chapter 1), and appeals until 1858 were handled through the courts' four-level hierarchical structure, as described above. In that year the Matrimonial Causes Act of 1857 [3.17] came into effect setting up a new temporal court in which, as in the case of probate, temporal lawyers were empowered to act.

Ecclesiastical peculiars

Some 300 *Peculiars* and *Donatives*, which were areas exempt from the jurisdiction of an archdeacon or a bishop, also crossed the four-level hierarchical ecclesiastical court system. The judicial role in a peculiar was exercised either by the Crown, or an archbishop, another diocesan bishop, a prebend, Chapters of a cathedral or collegiate church, individual Chapter members, the incumbent of a parish, the mayor of a town, the lord of a manor or a corporate body such as a university. Some peculiars were also *Liberties* or *Sokes*, areas exempt by a Royal grant from the jurisdiction of the Crown, although by no means was every Liberty a peculiar. The Dissolution of the Monasteries caused the demise of many peculiars, some of which had been under the jurisdiction of a monastery or abbey, although when the Royal Commission on Ecclesiastical Courts was preparing its report in 1831 [3.18] there were still some in every diocese: York had 52, Lichfield 37 and there were 45 incumbents in Winchester who each had his own court. By this time, however, the business con-ducted in the peculiar courts was concerned almost entirely with probate, and during the nineteenth century many peculiars were merged with normal parishes or became such in their own right. Appeal from a peculiar court generally went direct to the archbishop; although from the peculiar of an incumbent, or of a lord of a manor, appeal was to a bishop's court.

In the province of Canterbury there was a separate *Court of Peculiars* which dealt with all matters in the parishes within certain deaneries over which the bishops had no jurisdiction, for example those of London, Rochester and Winchester.

A Donative was somewhat similar to a peculiar in being a parish exempt from the jurisdiction of an archdeacon or bishop. However, in a Donative the incumbent could be appointed by the patron without reference to the bishop. Donatives were abolished by the 1818 Benefices Act [3.19].

4. Archbishops' Courts

Provinces of Canterbury and York

Historically (and until 1923, when the ecclesiastical province of Wales was created) there were only two provinces in England and Wales [4.1], namely Canterbury in the south and York in the north. For the purposes of administration, most of Wales and the Channel Islands were included in Canterbury, and the Isle of Man in the York province. In both ecclesiastical provinces an abundance of archiepiscopal courts evolved to cope with an archbishop's many duties and responsibilities. These courts were not totally dissimilar from those described in Chapter 3, though in the two provinces their development, organisation, and nomenclature were rarely identical. In general, the ecclesiastical courts in the northern province disliked any dictates from the south and, using every ruse to ignore successive Archbishops of Canterbury on all possible occasions, followed procedures more akin to civil law than ecclesiastical law which was adhered to more rigorously in the southern province.

Until 1835 there were five dioceses in the York Province compared with 23 in the Canterbury Province; see the map on page 36. Even with fewer courts in York some officials held the same post in more than one court; hence those officials often conducted the businesses of different courts on the same occasion. This also enabled junior officials in one court to be promoted to a senior position in another court. Whilst this was, perhaps, convenient for them, it created difficulties in adhering to strict procedures and recording court business. Details on the surviving records of all ecclesiastical courts, and their whereabouts, are given in Chapter 10.

Consistory Court

Because each archbishop was additionally the bishop of a diocese within his province he had a Consistory Court (as did every bishop). In the southern province, the Consistory court for the diocese of Canterbury was termed the *Court of the Commissary General*. In the northern province the court exercising jurisdiction over the diocese of York was, more logically, termed simply the *Consistory Court*; during a vacancy the Court of the Dean and Chapter of York exercised jurisdiction. In the diocese of York the Consistory Court was often referred to as the *Archbishop's Court* or *Curia Eboracensis*, possibly because, until at least the late seventeenth century, it also acted as an appeal court - see Court of the Province, below. This has led to some subsequent misinterpretation, and mis-filing of data, for it was only within York diocese, and not in Carlisle, Chester or Durham Dioceses, that the Archbishop of York could really claim any "ownership" of a consistory court.

Exchequer Court

This court existed only in the Province of York - an example of the temporal leanings in the northern province. The Exchequer Court, although the responsibility of the archbishop, was invariably presided over by his representative, a Receiver-General, who acted originally as chief financial officer for the province. The Receiver-General joined other officials in being a senior administrative officer for the whole province, but gradually he took on other tasks on behalf of the archbishop. Hence much work that was done in other courts in the southern province was undertaken in the Exchequer Court of York in the north, including the granting of probate. In fact, this court later came to be best known for its testamentary activities. In this regard the Exchequer Court acted as a Consistory Court for example, from 1374, in granting probate of those having *bona notabilia* solely in York diocese. And there was some logic in this for the Archbishop of York was also Bishop of York Diocese. However, the Exchequer Court was also held in conjunction with the provincial Prerogative Court, as described in the following section.

Prerogative Court

Each province had a probate court, the Prerogative or *Testamentary Court* with jurisdiction over the entire province. The wills in the Prerogative Court of Canterbury (PCC) series begin in 1384 but the court itself was probably not formed until 1443. Initially the PCC sat at Lambeth Palace, but after the Reformation sat in Doctors' Commons (see Chapter 7). The Prerogative Court of York (PCY) was not established until 1577 and probate was mostly granted in the Exchequer Court of York before and after then. In fact, for a considerable period of time, the Prerogative Court and the Exchequer Court appear to have worked together in this province and wills from both were registered together - although separate Act Books were maintained, certainly after 1624.

Court of the Province

Each province had a general appeal court, in some cases simply called the Court of the Province. In the Province of Canterbury this court acquired the title *Court of Arches* or *Supreme Court of Appeal*, while in the Province of York the corresponding court was called the *Chancery Court* of York, yet another example of the temporal inclinations in this province, although appeals here could alternatively be heard in the Consistory Court of York until the late seventeenth century.

The Canterbury provincial court derived its name from the Church of St Mary-le-Bow, nicknamed St Mary the Arches because of its arched vaultings, where it had sat from 1280. The peculiar court of St Mary, and of twelve other City of London parishes, also sat here. Unfortunately most of the early records of the Court of Arches have been lost (see Chapter 10).

The Chancery Court of York operated differently from the Court of Arches in several respects: in dealing with appeals from the Prerogative Court, the Chancery Court retained only grants and decrees, returning original probate documents to the Prerogative Court. In addition, the Chancery Court doubled-up as the Court of Audience (see below) in the northern province and also dealt with a variety of causes, such as defamation (on many occasions in the early seventeenth century), presentments, and those causes from promoted, and *ex officio*, cases (see Chapter 2). Furthermore, the Chancery Court granted probate of deceased beneficed clergy having goods in only one jurisdiction in the northern province (which one would have expected to have been dealt with at diocesan level - see Chapter 3), as well as of most clergy having goods in more than one jurisdiction (logical for an archbishop's court); from 1822 probate of such clergy was granted in the PCY.

Court of Audience

Each province had a Court of Audience, where the archbishop himself, or an auditor on his behalf, heard cases almost on a personal basis, not by way of appeal but by way, in the first instance, of complaint. In 1660, at the Restoration of the Monarchy, the Court of Audience in the Province of Canterbury was merged with the Consistory Court of St Paul's Cathedral which was, in effect, the Court of Arches. In York, however, its Audience Court was often held in conjunction with the Chancery Court.

Court for the Trial of Heresy

Each province had a Court for the Trial of Heresy, dealing with cases direct from anywhere within its responsibility, if necessary overlooking the protocol of seeking the bishop's consent, so important was the aim to stamp out heresy. There were, in addition, other routes for dealing with heretics, outlined in Chapters 2 and 3, and in the northern province there is no evidence for this court being separately convened.

Convocation

Each province had a *Convocation of the Province* which was, and is, a seminar of clergy from the province called by their archbishop on behalf of the monarch. Strictly, all Convocations are called only by Royal Writ. Some of the most important ecclesiastical documents - the Canons - originated in, and were passed by, Convocations of the Provinces, but see page 78. In the Province of Canterbury the organisation of Convocation was based on the English Parliamentary system with an Upper and a Lower House. In recent years the chief officer in the Upper House has been termed *President*, while in the Lower House he has been known, for centuries, as *Prolocutor*. The archbishop and bishops sat in the Upper House, while in the Lower House sat the deans, archdeacons, and proctors (see Chapter 5) - the latter having been elected by the Chapters and parochial clergy as their representatives. In the very early Convocations in Canterbury, and throughout their entire operational existence in York, there was only one House. For the Canterbury Convocation, in each diocese the Chapter chose one proctor while the beneficed clergy chose two proctors. For the York Convocation (York Province had fewer dioceses than Canterbury, as mentioned above) the beneficed clergy in each archdeaconry chose two proctors. The composition of the Convocations was changed in 1936.

Convocation acted in judicial matters, certainly in the fourteenth and fifteenth centuries. In the Lollard trials, and in early Convocations, the archbishop pronounced judgment on proven cases of heresy passed to him by a bishop; an interesting eighteen-page *Account of the proceedings in Convocation in a cause of Contumacy, commenc'd 10 April 1707* by Bishop Edmund Gibson was published that year. In 1842 Thomas Lathbury wrote a useful, but somewhat ponderous, history of the Convocation to 1742; this was republished in 1853 [4.2]. R R Pearce's *Law Relating to Convocation of the Clergy...* [4.3], published in 1848, explains legal issues and procedures followed in Convocations.

Convocation was (and strictly, still is) able to legislate by issuing canons under licence from the Crown (although the *General Synod of the Church of England* has acted for Convocation since 1970 - as explained on page 78), but this right has rarely been exercised in the past two hundred years. In 1937, however, the Lower House of the Convocation of York passed a resolution to review the Canons of 1603. In 1939 the Lower House of Canterbury proposed that a Commission be established to examine this. As a result the Archbishops of Canterbury and York appointed a Commission to prepare a revised body of Canons; these were finally implemented in 1969, as has been described in Chapter 1. Although nowadays the General Synod has the power to formulate Canons, they still require the Royal Assent.

Court for the Trial of Bishops
Each province had a Court for the Trial of Bishops although the power of the court, and its existence in York, was not readily accepted. This court (its terms of reference were confirmed by the 1840 Church Discipline Act) remained distinct from the Court of Audience. The archbishop himself presided over these cases but he had his Official Principal at his elbow and a number of bishops as Assessors; notwithstanding, even the archbishop's judgment was challenged on occasions.

Other Archiepiscopal Courts
Two further archbishops' courts, the provincial court set up by the Benefices Act (1898), to hear causes concerning bishops who refused potential clergy being presented to benefices, and the court established by the Bishops' (Retirement) Measure of 1951 have been referred to in Chapter 2.

5. Ecclesiastical Judges

Official, Commissary & Auditor

The ecclesiastical courts, apart from the Papal Court, were initially presided over personally by the archbishop, bishop or archdeacon (as appropriate), with experienced clerics in attendance. From about 1150 a cleric with such a background was commissioned (empowered to act) as a surrogate judge on behalf of the archbishop (or bishop or archdeacon) and usually termed the *Official* or *Commissary* - except in the peculiar courts of the prebendaries of York, and later in the Chancery Court of York, where a surrogate judge was often termed an *Auditor*.

The ecclesiastical judge had to be in holy orders (but not necessarily a priest - those in minor orders, for example deacons, were acceptable) and over twenty-five years of age [5.1]. He was fully competent in canon law in terms of his education, experience and training - in fact he had read for a degree in canon law at university and was skilled in its practical application. He was commissioned more or less on a fixed contract for a limited period, or during the bishop's pleasure, to hear a defined number of cases. In theory this meant that if a new bishop took over, the judge could not remain in office until that new bishop had drawn up a fresh contract; in practice, however, the judge often continued to act - similarly to a parish clerk who, though appointed by one parson, continued to serve a successor.

Official Principal, Commissary General & Dean

From the thirteenth century a cleric was allocated permanently to a specific court as its judge and was termed the *Official Principal* or *Commissary General* and the diocesan court was usually termed a *Consistory Court*. Whereas in the Province of Canterbury the Consistory Court of the Canterbury Diocese was presided over by a Commissary General, in the Archbishop's peculiars of other dioceses, the judge was termed a *Dean*. As an Official Principal the surrogate ecclesiastical judge was empowered with identical authority to that of the bishop; thus any appeals against his decisions were referred directly to an archbishop, not to a bishop, as the Official Principal was already acting for the bishop as his equal.

The judge of the peculiar court of St Mary-le-Bow (St Mary the Arches) in London was called the *Dean of Arches*. Towards the end of the thirteenth century, as mentioned in Chapter 4, the Canterbury provincial appeal court sat in St Mary-le-Bow church. In a staff-cutting exercise in about 1510, when the same individual acted as judge of both the peculiar court and the provincial court, the Official

Principal of the Court of Canterbury became known by the more attractive title of Dean of Arches, even though his work in the peculiar court was less prestigious.

Vicar-General & Chancellor

Bishops, especially when away from their dioceses, also deputed clerics to perform, on their behalf, other non-judicial duties such as granting licences or dispensations and giving institution to benefices (inducting a priest to a specific parish); a cleric acting in this capacity was termed *Vicar-General*. Over the years the latter became a permanent post and was often held by the Official Principal. From the mid-sixteenth century the person who exercised both offices was known in most courts as a *Chancellor*, though acting as Vicar-General when dealing with non-judicial matters and as Official Principal when passing sentences in the Consistory Court. This was a marked change from former times when a Chancellor had been little more than a secretary or personal assistant to the bishop. The judge in some courts, as already mentioned above, was called a Dean in preference to Chancellor, whilst in others he was known as an Auditor or a Commissary General.

Commissary, Master & Keeper

In the testamentary or probate courts of the archbishops the judges were termed variously *Commissaries*, *Masters* or *Keepers*; in the Exchequer Court of York, for example, the judge was called a Commissary and yet also acted as *Receiver-General* on behalf of the archbishop for exchequer matters.

President & Prolocutor

In each of the Convocations, as mentioned in Chapter 4, the chief officer in the Upper House is termed President - equivalent to the Lord Chancellor in the House of Lords. In the Lower House the chief officer is termed Prolocutor - the equivalent of The Speaker in the House of Commons.

Other judges

Various titles were used for judges acting in other courts on behalf of the archbishops in the provinces of Canterbury and York. In the Canterbury Court, after the 1533 Ecclesiastical Licences Act (as the Act of Dispensation, or Peter's Pence Act is sometimes called) [5.2], the Official Principal should have been formally termed Dean of Arches, Vicar-General of the Province of Canterbury (confirming the election of bishops) and Master of the Faculties (granting dispensations and creating notaries public for the whole of England); and following the 1874 Public Worship Regulation Act [5.3] he was also Auditor of the Court of York. The 1874 Act required the same person to be Official Principal of both provinces - although the Ecclesiastical Fees Act of 1875 [5.4] enabled the Vicar-General of York and the Auditor to be separate persons.

Appointing judges

In the early seventeenth century [5.5] a bishop granted the two offices of Official Principal and Vicar-General to an individual by letters patent for life - there were no appointments by commission and no time restrictions - and these were ratified by the Dean and Chapter of the diocesan cathedral. In other words, the practice that had been followed for over 500 years, of having a commissioned cleric under a fixed contract, was phased out. This policy created the situation whereby a judge, once in post, could not be removed from office, although a bishop still had the right to sit as judge himself in his own court if he so wished. Nevertheless, the situation was developing whereby the bishops' appointees were becoming more closely associated with the bishops' courts than were the bishops themselves. This association had begun in 1545 [5.6] when laymen and doctors of civil law became eligible for appointment as ecclesiastical judges and the bishops began to become distanced from the everyday procedures in the ecclesiastical courts. In practice Chancellors tended to be clergymen, while judges of the more important ecclesiastical courts were exclusively laymen, generally from Doctors' Commons (see Chapter 7).

Judges' qualifications

From 1603 [5.7] it was a requirement (although sometimes ignored) for ecclesiastical judges to be at least twenty-six years of age, to be competent in Civil (Roman) Law as well as in Canon Law (especially to be able to deal with probate and matrimonial causes), and to subscribe to the Thirty Nine Articles. Under Canon 128 the surrogate or deputy ecclesiastical judge mentioned above, who was appointed to keep court during the judge's absence, had to meet certain conditions: he was required to be (although this also was sometimes ignored) a grave minister and a graduate, or a licensed public preacher and a beneficed man near the place where the court was kept, or to be a Bachelor of Law or a Master of Arts skilled in Civil and Canon Law.

Post - Reformation Dioceses (1541 - 1835)

6. Other Ecclesiastical Court Officials

Besides the judges identified in Chapter 5, other officials were needed in the ecclesiastical courts having a thorough understanding of canon (and civil) law to enable the complexities of the ecclesiastical legal system to operate successfully. There were two groups of ecclesiastical lawyers: proctors and advocates.

Proctor

A *proctor* undertook duties equivalent to those of a solicitor or common law attorney in the temporal, common law, courts, although the proctor was originally in a separate branch of the legal profession, not merely a solicitor with authority in the ecclesiastical courts. (The word proctor is a contraction of prolocutor but these two positions had different responsibilities.) He normally held a first (Bachelor's) degree and had to be formally admitted by the judge of the church court. In very many situations proctors acted in the ecclesiastical courts quite contrary to canon law, by undertaking roles that legally were open only to advocates. In most courts Canons 130 and 131 relating to this seem to have been totally ignored, as described in Chapter 8. By 1832 there were 109 proctors in courts in Canterbury and London, eight in York and two or three in smaller diocesan courts. Their numbers dwindled so drastically as the ecclesiastical courts closed that in 1877 the Solicitors Act [6.1] had to be introduced, permitting solicitors to practise as proctors in the few remaining church courts.

Advocate

An *advocate* undertook duties equivalent to those of counsel or a barrister in the common law courts. Normally holding a Doctorate (Doctor's degree), his formal admittance by the judge of the court was based on a fiat - written authorisation - from the Archbishop of Canterbury. The majority of the advocates, as described in Chapter 7, practised in the Provincial Court of Canterbury and the Consistory Court of London although, as mentioned above, they should have exercised a far wider remit. Both of these courts had the same group of advocates (there were eighteen of them in 1832), all of whom were members of Doctors' Commons, the complexities of which are described in Chapter 7. Prior to the Reformation most advocates, after their formal authorisation, practised in the Court of Arches, although the Provincial Court of York also had advocates. The majority of advocates came from "substantial" backgrounds (their families had to maintain them well into their 30s) and even if their fathers were not armigerous most advocates, certainly by the eighteenth century, were themselves granted arms. The profession, as was the case with many another, attracted other members from the same family and a significant number were sons or nephews of advocates or proctors.

Apparitor

Apparitors or *Summoners* were appointed by the judge of an ecclesiastical court to keep order and serve notices of the court on those concerned, acting similarly to beadles who operated at the parochial level. However, it would seem in 1603 at least that apparitors were used as "diocesan policemen" [6.2] to keep churchwardens informed of offenders in their parish, thereby enabling the churchwardens to present those offenders at a Visitation. These apparitors also were expected to send quarterly reports to the bishop of causes that were faltering, of penances commuted for a cash payment, of names of recusants, heretics, schismatics and non-resident incumbents, to send details on unlawful marriages, sequestrations and the lack of sermons, information on chancels and parsonages requiring repairs and on charitable legacies. They were also to inform the bishop about the death of an incumbent, within six days of the event, and of the name of the executor or administrator 14 days after the death of a testator. Some of these activities obviously provided interim intelligence pending the distribution of the next Articles of Enquiry.

Apparitor General, Examiner, Scribe & Registrar

By 1328, *Apparitors General* were being appointed in York, in a supervisory role over the other apparitors for the courts under their jurisdiction, on a fixed-term contract basis but by the end of the century appointment was for life. An Apparitor General is mentioned in the courts of the Prior and Chapter of Canterbury from 1442. This does not appear to have been a full-time job and the Apparitor General was also appointed as the Registrar (see below). In the diocese of Canterbury the names of apparitors responsible for citations from 1454 were entered in the consistory and archidiaconal books at the beginning of the Act (account of court business) relating to the suit. To serve the various notices, the apparitors had to travel throughout the area for which the court had responsibility, although the deanery apparitors in Canterbury were forbidden to use horses as a method of transport [6.3].

Examiners were appointed in some courts as officials whose main duties were to question or examine the parties or their representatives. Examiners' fees were very clearly established. Each court also had a *Scribe* who wrote up the proceedings, and a *Clerk* or *Registrar* who was officially responsible for the court records; the latter was also a Master of Arts and Notary Public, appointed for administrative ability rather than legal expertise, whose office originated in 1215 [6.4] when two honest witnesses were appointed by the judge of a court to keep its Acts. From the seventeenth century Registrars were appointed for life under letters patent from the bishop, confirmed by the Dean and Chapter of the diocese. On appointment a Registrar took the same oath and made the same declaration as prescribed (by Canon 127) for an ecclesiastical judge. Many courts also had Deputy Registrars.

Secretary, Sealer & Record Keeper

Part of the work for some courts was undertaken by an archbishop's or bishop's *Secretary*, some licences and agreements were formally sealed by a *Sealer* or *Seal Keeper* and records not registered by the Registrar were maintained by a *Record Keeper*. These officials were entitled to fees, later fixed by Acts of Parliament.

Officials' standards

It is obvious from Canons 127 to 138 that in the early seventeenth century the quality of all the ecclesiastical court officials was below acceptable standards and in need of considerable improvement. A minimum age and academic achievements were identified for the judges and their surrogates in Canons 127 and 128. Restrictions were placed on proctors in Canons 129 to 133, and their work effectively required to be overseen by advocates. Proctors were far too unruly for the establishment; as Canon 133 pointed out, "the loud and confused cries and clamours of proctors in the courts of the Archbishop are not only troublesome and offensive to the Judges and Advocates, but also give occasion to the standers-by, of contempt and calumny toward the court itself". The Canon went on to require the proctors to "refrain loud speech and babbling, and behave themselves quietly and modestly; and that when either the Judges or Advocates, or any of them shall happen to speak, they presently be silent, upon pain of silencing for two whole terms then immediately following every offence of theirs. And if any of them shall the second time offend therein, and after due monition shall not reform himself, let him be for ever removed from his practice". Firm measures were needed for this group of ecclesiastical court lawyers who had obviously got well out of hand over many years.

They were not alone, however, in letting standards slip: Canon 134 refers to the Registrars and their Deputies failing to keep the court records correctly, not preparing the citations, not ensuring that witnesses were available for questioning, failing to register wills within a reasonable time, falsifying in, and omitting information from, the records, and receiving bribes from various parties. Any of these shortcomings could result in a one, two or three month suspension, or even longer, and running the risk of being replaced by another Notary Public. Several officials were taking fees that were too high and Canons 135 to 137 attempted to restrain this practice. Canon 138 sought to suppress the huge numbers of overpaid apparitors, themselves surrounded by armies of messengers and substitutes employed in the ecclesiastical courts; by this Canon the bishops and their deputies were required to reduce numbers and, if they were not ruthless enough, the Archbishop of Canterbury was to use his discretion as a hatchet man.

After the Reformation the Court of High Commission and the High Court of Delegates, which were both senior to the Provincial Courts (although the Court of High Commission was not an appellate court), drew their judges from different categories of persons from those in the courts mentioned above or, indeed, from those in their own courts. The members of the Court of High Commission were bishops or other clergy, common law and ecclesiastical judges and civil servants. At ordinary sittings of this court the commissioners were usually clergymen and ecclesiastical judges. The High Court of Delegates comprised solely advocates from Doctors' Commons (and so were ecclesiastical lawyers) prior to 1640; but between 1640 and 1750 the ecclesiastical lawyers were joined by bishops and common law judges. From 1750 the Court comprised three common law judges and four or five advocates.

Convocation, from a 15th Century Manuscript

7. Doctors' Commons

Origins

The greatest concentration of advocates was in the City of London: those at the Court of Arches (which sat at St Mary-le-Bow, as explained in Chapter 4), those at the Prerogative Court of Canterbury dealing with probate (which sat at St Paul's Cathedral or in the Prerogative Court's own chambers in Ivy Lane), and those at the Court of the Dean and Chapter of St Paul's. It was, therefore, only natural that many of the Doctors of Law should come together as a Society in a "collegiate manner" for social and professional intercourse; this was similar to the subsequent gatherings of the *Chemical Society* in Burlington House or the earlier *Jesus Commons* - a college of priests in Dowgate, also in the City of London. Hence the building in Paternoster Row, in which the advocates congregated and enjoyed some accommodation, derived its name from the priests' college and by 1496 had become known as Doctors' Commons. Many other organisations, whose members enjoyed a common interest or shared common dining or cultural facilities, also established Commons or Common Rooms.

Members

Not a few advocates chose not to pay the annual 6s.8d. subscription to join Doctors' Commons (6s.8d. and 13s.4d. were extensively-applied costs in the past for many goods and services, being one third and two thirds of a pound sterling - or a half-Mark and one Mark - as described in the Cameo *How Heavy, How Much and How Long?* [7.1]); whereas in contrast a number of non-practising members with strong ecclesiastical connections did join the Society, evidently to enjoy the hospitality provided. Geoffrey Blythe, Bishop of Coventry and Lichfield, was the first of several out-of-town members who found the lodgings useful when attending London meetings; John Colet, Dean of St Paul's Cathedral, was one of a number of members working nearby who also joined, obviously finding the club atmosphere congenial. A Subscription Book for members of Doctors' Commons was started in 1511, incorporating data from an earlier record; this book lists names of members, including some who did not pay their annual subscriptions, and continued in use until 1855. A profusely annotated transcript of the book was published, with a comprehensive commentary by G D Squibb, in 1977 [7.2]. Details of other records of Society members and staff are given in Chapter 10 of this Cameo.

In 1531 the first advocate not to have been in even minor orders was admitted as a member of Doctors' Commons; and from 1532, when Henry VIII began his formal severance from Rome and appeals from ecclesiastical courts ceased to be referred to the Pope (see Chapter 3), in-depth expertise on Roman canon law was no longer required. This, in turn, meant that thereafter clerical advocates were not essential, thereby enabling ecclesiastical lawyers and married laymen to exercise ecclesiastical jurisdiction. As the sixteenth century progressed and clerical advocates moved from the courts into ecclesiastical posts, or died while still practising, they were replaced by laymen. The Court of High Commission, as mentioned above, emerged in 1580 as the appeal court replacing the Papal Court. The last proctor had been admitted to Doctors' Commons in 1569 and the last time an ordained man was admitted to Doctors' Commons as an advocate was in 1609. In fact by 1747 it was confirmed that an advocate who took holy orders could not practise in the courts at Doctors' Commons; and the Court of the King's Bench further decided in 1807 that someone already ordained could not become an advocate. Even by 1600 the advocates were no longer clergymen spending some "time out" from pastoral and clerical duties to gain experience by practising in the ecclesiastical courts, but were full-time legal practitioners with careers as lay, but professional, civil lawyers.

However, in the early sixteenth century the members of Doctors' Commons held Doctorates from Oxford, Cambridge or European universities, notably in Italy, causing their average age to be at least 30. Many of those with foreign degrees were incorporated at Oxford or Cambridge, but not necessarily so as can be seen by scrutiny of the Subscription Book.

Move to Mountjoy House

Doctors' Commons, as a name for the club or Society, and for the building it occupied, was retained when the Doctors of Law moved in 1568 from Paternoster Row to Mountjoy House in Knightrider Street; this property was owned by the Dean and Chapter of St Paul's Cathedral. The move was facilitated by Dr Henry Hervey, Master of Trinity Hall, Cambridge who was, himself, a member of Doctors' Commons. Having such learned men on their premises was too good an opportunity for the Dean and Chapter to miss; accordingly the terms of the ninety-nine year lease of Mountjoy House to the Master, Fellows and Scholars of Trinity Hall, not only permitted the "Advocates and Doctors of the Court of Arches in London and others of that Company and Commons learned men graduates of the Universities" to live there, but required the advocates to "freely give their best advice and counsel concerning the ecclesiastical laws of the realm, should the Dean and Chapter need it". Regarding accommodation, single advocates took priority, followed by married advocates, any further doctors of law and then other graduate members of the Society - although no wives were permitted to lodge or abide there at this time. (Married advocates gradually moved into properties nearby.) The Master of Trinity

Hall was provided with two chambers whilst nineteen other tenants were provided with rooms either on 21-year sub-leases from Trinity Hall or one-year sub-tenancies. But the Knightrider property did not have infinite capacity and on 25 June 1579, on account of the "limitations of the common table and of the linen", it was resolved to admit no more members until the number fell to twenty; preference was to be given to senior advocates in the order of their admission to the Court of Arches. Within three years death and retirement had alleviated the situation and any advocate was again eligible such that in October 1585, and in January and April 1586, special resolutions were needed to admit friends and relations of senior members. It was not until the 1593 Michaelmas Term that the limit in membership of Doctors' Commons was raised from 20 to 33. For example, Henry Hickman [7.3], who had been admitted to the Court of Arches on 9 May 1586 was not admitted a member of Doctors' Commons until 14 May 1595.

Relocation

The name Doctors' Commons was further extended as time went by to the courts, even to the Prerogative Court of Canterbury, in which the advocates practised and also to the whole neighbourhood where the officers of the courts were housed. Sadly, the Knightrider property came to an untimely end on 3 September 1666 when it was destroyed in the Great Fire of London. Luckily two of its important records, the Subscription Book and the Long Book (see Chapter 10 for a description of their content), were rescued on the following day; and in October of that year the Society took up temporary, but extremely comfortable, residence in Exeter House opposite the Savoy in the Strand. The Court of Arches, dislodged by the additional destruction of St Mary-le-Bow, was most conveniently also housed in Exeter House.

So comfortable were the advocates in Exeter House that when the Doctors' Commons premises were rebuilt on the Knightrider site in 1670-72, they had to be enticed into returning by exempting them from the obligation to hold any office in that ward and, on intervention from the King, the obligation to hold any office in the City of London. Nineteen sets of chambers of varying sizes were designed for residential occupation; thus wives and families, including servants, moved in with some of the advocates, who held new leases of forty years from Trinity Hall with a covenant for a new lease for forty years after the expiration of sixteen years. The rebuilt Doctors' Commons also contained a court room so that the appellate Court of Arches could be held on their premises - a convenience they had enjoyed at Exeter House. The court room was used also by the Court of Admiralty, the Prerogative Court of Canterbury and the Consistory Court of the Bishop of London.

The lease held by Trinity Hall was due to expire in 1730, but subject to a covenant for constant renewal. However, when negotiations began in 1725 the Dean and

Chapter of St Paul's claimed that they could not grant a lease in a city for more than forty years. Thus the ninety-nine year lease of 1568 was invalid. After proceedings in the Court of Chancery and an appeal to the House of Lords a compromise was reached for Doctors' Commons to have a new lease for forty years from 1730, but with no covenant for renewal. Not wishing to be evicted in 1770 the advocates filed a Bill in Chancery in 1765 against the Dean and Chapter; when these proceedings were heard in 1767 the case was dismissed. This prompted the advocates to petition for a Royal Charter - which they were granted on 22 June 1768. Having become a body corporate the advocates were able to negotiate directly with the Dean and Chapter without Trinity Hall as the intermediary, and they were able to extend their lease to 1810. Knowing even this to be somewhat precarious they managed to secure the freehold of the property in 1783, but only through a complicated mortgage arrangement and with a substantial cash grant from the Crown.

Decline

By the second decade of the nineteenth century the advocates themselves and their very existence, or at least the activities of the ecclesiastical courts, were being questioned yet again. A Royal Commission to inquire into the Church Courts was set up in January 1820 but this was postponed as a result of the death of George III. The report in 1832 of the reconvened Commission was noted only, without any action being taken, and it seemed that the courts and Doctors' Commons were being spared. However, the returns to the Commission showed that the vast majority of judges of the Consistory Courts were clergymen with no formal legal training whatsoever; only six were members of Doctors' Commons, and one was a barrister. It was no wonder that some authorities, if only between themselves, were wondering if advocates were really needed. But Parliament was not to remain oblivious for ever and an Act [7.4] of 1836, the outcome of two other Royal Commissions which had been set up to consider the state of the dioceses in England and Wales, managed to incorporate some analysis of the church courts and hinted at changes to come. A fleeting glimpse of life at Doctors' Commons at this period in time can be gleaned by reading Charles Dickens' semi-autobiographical *David Copperfield.*

Temporary Acts maintained the status quo until 1853 when George Hadfield introduced a Bill into Parliament to transfer the granting of probate to the common law and county courts. The Bill did not proceed and in the next session of Parliament another Bill proposed that probate be transferred to the Court of Chancery. This also failed, possibly because the advocates within Doctors' Commons, sensing the immediacy of the situation, began not only to make plans for the disposal of their real and personal property by letting, sale or exchange, but drew the attention of the House of Lords to their plight. Nevertheless, on 25 August 1857 the Court of Probate Act [7.5] abolished the testamentary jurisdiction of the ecclesiastical and other courts and provided that from 11 January 1858 such jurisdiction should be exercised by a new Court of Probate in which serjeants and barristers were authorised to practise in contentious matters. Henceforth appeals regarding probate were directed to the House of Lords. In compensation, the advocates, being civil lawyers from the ecclesiastical courts, were given the right to practise as common lawyers in any court in England and with the same eligibility to appointments as if they had been called to the Bar when they were admitted as advocates. They were also permitted to surrender the Charter of Doctors' Commons to the Crown, and so the property and chattels passed to the members in equal share. In the event, the advocates' monopoly of non-contentious business lasted for less than a year as the 1858 Court of Probate Act [7.6] entitled serjeants and barristers to practise in all causes and matters in the Court of Probate.

On 28 August 1857 the Court of Divorce and Matrimonial Causes was established by the Matrimonial Causes Act 1857 [7.7], in which advocates and barristers would practise. The 1857 Court of Probate Act provided there should be one judge in the Probate Court, who was later also appointed Judge Ordinary of the Court of Divorce and Matrimonial Causes. A Principal Registry was to serve both courts and was attached to the Court of Probate·in London, and simultaneously to District Registries across the remainder of England and Wales. The same Court of Probate Act also provided that judgeships of the Court of Probate and the High Court of Admiralty could be united at the next vacancy (although the opportunity for this did not occur until 1863). On 8 August 1859 another Act [7.8] enabled serjeants, barristers, attorneys and solicitors to practise in the Court of Admiralty.

The advocates were left with only the Court of Arches as their exclusive domain, but even this was subtly phased out and in 1867 a barrister was, for the first of many subsequent occasions, permitted to sign articles which were, by the Church Discipline Act 1840 [7.9], strictly required to be signed by an ecclesiastical lawyer, that is an advocate practising in Doctors' Commons. By the Supreme Court of Judicature Act in 1873 [7.10], the Court for Divorce and Matrimonial Causes was brought together with the Court of Probate and the High Court of Admiralty in the Probate, Divorce and Admiralty Division and their jurisdiction was transferred to the High Court of the Supreme Court.

Disposal of assets

After a number of attempts from 1858 to dispose of Doctors' Commons, the property was finally sold on 24 June 1865 to the Metropolitan Board of Works; two years later the Board demolished the buildings and sold off the materials as part of the Thames Embankment Scheme and an associated feeder road. In 1859 it had been proposed that the books in the Doctors' Commons Library be offered to the libraries of the Middle Temple and other Inns of Court but this was not pursued. The book collection was finally sold in 1861, about one third being bought by the government for the Court of Admiralty and the Court of Probate; those books are now in the Supreme Court Library at the Central Law Courts, Lincoln's Inn, London. The remainder was sold at auction to other purchasers.

Although the corporate body was enabled by the 1857 Probate Act to surrender its charter, Doctors' Commons actually continued to exist in law as an entity until the last member, Dr Tristam, who still held the Charter itself, died on 8 March 1921. His son subsequently presented the document to All Souls College, Oxford for preservation.

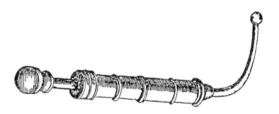

Ecclesiastically-licensed midwives were encouraged to baptise sickly children, in the womb if necessary using a Baptismal Syringe, such as this one designed by François Mauriceau in the 17th Century.

8. Ecclesiastical Court Procedures

For causes where there were no disputes, arguments or appeals, such as the granting of probate in non-controversial or non-correctional cases, the issuing of licences for matrimonial purposes or for preachers, or schoolmasters, or midwives or surgeons, the ecclesiastical court procedures were relatively simple; the events were merely entered into Muniment Books or Registers or Act Books, and any sums of cash taken as fees were recorded in those or in separate account books. Where a court official (see Chapter 6) was acting on behalf, say, of an archbishop, the *fiat* (the authority) for him to do so was normally attached to the documentation.

If any of the above or similar causes were disputed or contested, a plethora of documentation could result, as it did if the Church, or indeed an individual, felt there was some charge to be brought against another party. Whatever the situation, a log book or journal was kept as a record of the court deliberations or business; this was traditionally called a *Liber Actorum* (Act Book), although other terms were also used.

Anyone, apart from an excommunicate or an outlaw, could start a suit in an ecclesiastical court. From the early thirteenth century, the first step was to engage the services of an advocate (although in very many cases a proctor was engaged instead - see below) to act as a proxy throughout the suit, whether it was civil or criminal. Normally at this stage Letters of Proxy were drawn up in which the prosecutor and the defendant each named their advocates; they usually also named a reserve, in a substitution clause, should the first choice be unable to attend the court. Civil suits were known as Instance Cases and were *ad instantiam partis* (between party and party) and dealt with the moral principles or legal establishment of the Church; examples of civil suits were those that involved moving a pew or church seat, non-payment of church rates and granting of a faculty. Criminal suits, all brought *pro salute animae* (for the salvation of the soul), could normally proceed only if accepted by the ecclesiastical court judge (before the 13th Century the procedures seem to have been much more informal and paternalistic); examples of criminal suits were spiritual offences, proceedings to punish and reinstate a sinful offender by a public reprimand (judicial reprimand) or more severe punishment, and cases that involved church discipline. Criminal suits were known as Office Cases as they were promoted by the office of the judge (in the name of the bishop) and could be one of the following:

a) of his own motion, through information received from the office of the court;

b) from presentments of churchwardens or sidesmen at Visitations (see Chapters 1 and 2 - the presentments produced enormous numbers of suits, particularly in the archdeacons' courts);

c) promotions of another party (the promoter).

The court procedure in the above suits could be *Plenary* or *Summary*, and in a probate case the procedure was *Testamentary*.

Plenary procedure was used in all civil suits and in those criminal suits in which the office of the judge had been promoted. Cases were conducted almost entirely through written documents - and so are extremely useful for researchers today if the documentation has survived. As a consequence there was no public cross-examination, no arguments of counsel (and so no opportunity for eloquent professional speeches to be recorded), and the decisions of the court were based on rational interpretations of written evidence. The stages in plenary procedure are explained below. Summary procedure was used in criminal suits against those laity who had committed moral offences; the accused was brought before the judge and the first plea (the case for the prosecution) and the reply by the defence and statements of witnesses were all taken in open court. The *first plea* in the ecclesiastical courts was equivalent to a *declaration* in the common law courts or a *bill* in the equity courts. Summary procedure, the stages of which are also explained in detail below, was used extensively by the ecclesiastical authorities during their Visitations. Testamentary procedure is outlined towards the end of this Chapter.

Plenary court procedure

In the first three stages of the procedure, outlined below, the cases should have been argued in the ecclesiastical courts by advocates; and in the Court of Arches, the Prerogative Court of Canterbury and the Consistory Court of London they were. However, in ecclesiastical courts outside of London the work was undertaken mostly by proctors - even though Canons 130 and 131 expressly forbade them to do so without advocates. Hence in the following account, where relevant, the word proctor is added in square brackets after advocate.

The first stage in the plenary court *processus* (procedure) in an instance (civil) case was for the plaintiff's advocate [but often incorrectly a proctor] to issue the first plea as a *libel* in the form of a written statement on the case; the libel ran in the name of the plaintiff or his advocate. In an office (criminal) case the promoter had already prepared a *querela* or *informatio* requesting the judge to decree a *citation* or a *citation mandate* and prepare articles or *materia* (a precis of the accusation); the court judge then issued the *libel* or *allegation* (in a civil suit; in a criminal suit *articles* were issued) which was filed with the court. At this stage a slight complication could arise as it was possible for a *caveat* to be issued by another party to stop the suit proceeding further.

The second stage in the procedure, after the judge had *decreed* (had agreed the issue of) *the citation*, was for the citation to be taken or sent by an apparitor of the court on behalf of the *pars actrix* (plaintiff) to the *pars rea* (accused or defendant). If the latter could not be located, so that he could not be given the citation personally, *letters missive* or a *decree viis et modis* (using all possible ways and means) was obtained by the plaintiff's advocate [proctor] and it was taken by an apparitor to the incumbent of the accused's parish where the citation was read out in his parish church during the Communion Service, after the creed. The incumbent signed the citation to indicate he had published it and he sent it back to the judge of the court who had issued it, where it was filed. In later times the *decree viis et modis* was left at the accused's house, or last known residence, or fixed to the door of his parish church. If the accused did not respond to the citation, even though it could not be proved that he had received or heard it, he was regarded as being *contumacious* (in contempt of court), and so placed himself in a vulnerable position whereby he could be excommunicated. In such a situation a *schedule of excommunication* was sent to the parish church for it to be denunciated by the incumbent, signed and returned to the court for filing. At this point a *significavit* could be issued in which the spiritual authorities called upon the secular authorities to secure the arrest of the accused. If he was tracked down and apprehended he was subsequently dealt with accordingly. If the accused responded to the citation he also appointed an advocate [proctor] to act on his behalf.

The third stage in the plenary procedure was a decision by the court officials as to how the case should proceed and within what approximate time scales, based on the libel, articles or potential allegation. There was, using the terminology, a *contestation of the suit* or a *joining of issue*, the documentation following a form of words that was quite consistent for a particular court and reasonably similar between the various courts. As described above, in a civil suit the plaintiff's advocate [proctor] put in a libel in which he stated his case; in a criminal suit the articles were *promoted* (prepared) by the plaintiff's advocate [proctor] and given to the judge, who then *propounded the articles* (clarified the position in a written statement of numbered paragraphs). The defendant or accused then had to respond *seriatim* (point by point, or article by article), and in a *responsa personalia* could either deny or accept the truth of the facts as set out in the libel or articles. If there was a denial the libel or articles were thereafter termed *allegations*; in fact all pleas, after the first plea, were called allegations whether in plenary, summary or testamentary causes. At this point the plaintiff was given a *term probatory* to prove his case, by providing witnesses who could be *examined* (questioned) in writing. The questions were called *interrogatories*, the replies (also in writing but in practice verbatim copies of the evidence) were called *depositions*. Both these sets of documents were filed with the court and made available to both sides. The advocates [proctors] acting for the defendant could make *replications* or *excipiendo* (exceptions) to the witnesses and these were also filed. Additional *positions* to support the libel on one side, or the allegation on the other side, and *additional* or *declaratory exceptions* from either side could also be provided as further documentation and filed with the court. Documentary *exhibits*, such as copies of plans or title deeds, to support the libel or the allegation were sometimes produced and filed with the court. If in his *reponsa personalia* the accused or defendant accepted the facts as set out in the libel or articles, the case was obviously foreshortened and moved to the fourth stage; but it was still up to the plaintiff's advocate [proctor] to prove the facts - and so the documentation was not that much less than when there was a denial of the facts. When the judge decided that sufficient evidence had been produced, and all exceptions appeared to have been dealt with, he closed this stage by assigning *a term to propound all acts* to establish a reasonable deadline for ending the case. During this period both sides had to finalise their evidence. A *term to conclude* was then assigned after which no further evidence was permissible.

The fourth stage in the plenary court procedure was the pronouncement by the judge of the *definitive* (sometimes termed diffinitive) *sentence* on the basis of all the documents that had been produced. Examples of sentences on both clergy and laity are given in Chapter 9. The judge also entered a *Taxed Bill* or *Bill of Taxed Costs*, which outlined any fees that had been incurred and how they should be paid. This document was also filed.

Summary court procedure

Summary procedures were applied to criminal suits or mere office, corrective, cases as they were sometimes termed, which arose from an accusation, presentment, denunciation, information or inquisition. Many summary cases were heard during a Visitation and so recorded in the *Visitation Book* or *Liber Compertorum* (book of things found out), rather than in a separate Act Book. Even so, a case was normally preceded by the issue of a citation, as described above for plenary procedure. If several people were asked to attend or provide information, a general citation *quorum nomina* (naming them all) was issued. In 1641 summary procedures were altered by statute [8.1]; the situations before and after this date are described here.

Prior to 1641 an accused person was brought before an ecclesiastical judge in open court and the first plea, the case for the prosecution, was heard. In a summary case the first plea was termed *articles* because it ran in the name of the ecclesiastical judge who articled and objected against the defendant or respondent. The accused was made to answer on oath as to the truth of the charges articled against him; this was termed an *ex-officio oath* or an *oath against malice*. If the accused denied the truth of the charges, he had to clear himself by producing five, or in some cases six, friends or neighbours to act as *compurgators* who would swear on oath as to his innocence. Compurgation, for this reasons, was known as *Wager of Law*. If he did produce the compurgators who supported him, an *intimation of purgation* was filed and the case was dismissed. If he could not produce the compurgators, but his denial was accepted, he was declared innocent by the court. For criminal suits the ex-officio oath and the use of compurgators were abolished in 1641; this abolition was confirmed at the Restoration of the Monarchy by the Ecclesiastical Jurisdiction Act of 1661 [8.2].

After 1641, when the articles (the case for the prosecution) had been put before the court, the *responsions* (reply by the defence) were heard by the judge in open court. Then the *attestations* of the witnesses for the prosecution were heard, after which the defence began their *interrogatories*. These four phases were repeated if the defence put forward *Articles of Exception* (their case) resulting in further responsions and attestations. However, the use of the ex-officio oath had been abolished only in criminal suits, and even in those suits the courts continued to make the accused swear as to the truth of the *common fame* (report of the charges) and not as to the truth of the charges themselves. If the accused denied the fame he still had to produce compurgators to support his denial. If the accused refused to swear, this was regarded as a confession of guilt. A promoter who failed to establish the truth of the crime or the fame could be sued for defamation.

As in the plenary court procedures, the ecclesiastical judge pronounced *sentence* on the accused or defendant; in summary cases he normally did this by imposing a penance, in open court, but he still entered his *Bill of Taxed Costs*. A *schedule of penance* or *confession*, or possibly a *decree of commutation of penance* was drawn up after the sentence had been announced. The former was sent to the accused's parish incumbent who countersigned it after the penance had been performed, and returned it to the court to be filed.

Note that in the High Court of Delegates, particularly, only the sentence was published, not the reasons for reaching that conclusion. There was no tradition or doctrine of binding precedents and, anyway, the judges in the provincial and diocesan courts felt no obligations to heed decisions made in higher courts. No reports of cases in any ecclesiastical courts were published until the mid-eighteenth century.

From 1854 [8.3] the church courts were empowered to examine witnesses orally in open court. However, by this period, as mentioned in Chapter 2, some of the courts had already been closed and only a few had much opportunity to exercise this right.

Testamentary court procedure

When a person died the interested parties, normally the next-of-kin, looked to see if a will had been made which expressed the wishes of the deceased as to how his estate should be handled on his death. However, as mentioned in Chapter 6, if the local apparitor knew that the deceased had made a will, he may have already alerted a church court to the news of the death. The estate may have comprised *personalty*, often incorrectly termed personal estate (goods and chattels), or interests in *real estate* (land) or both; strictly, following the 1540 Statute of Wills [8.4], a *will* dealt with real estate, which was devisable, and a *testament* dealt with personalty, which was bequeathable. However, the term will was used rather loosely to include both real estate and personalty although the individual expressing his wishes in the document was called a *testator*. The will could be hand-written by the testator himself, in which case it was termed *holograph*, or it could have been declared verbally, known as a *nuncupative* will: the 1678 Statute of Frauds required this to be made in the testator's own home, during his dying illness, and heard by at least three witnesses who were to arrange for the words to be written down within six days; after 14 days they had to confirm this at a probate court. After the 1837 Wills Act [8.5] a verbal will was valid only if made by a soldier on active service or by a seaman or mariner at sea.

If a will was found, the *executor* (*executrix* if a woman) or executors identified by the testator in the will took it, or an authenticated copy of it, to an ecclesiastical court, mindful that unless the effects were worth less than £5 the court, from 1529, was likely to charge a fee for granting probate. The choice for the appropriate court has already been explained in Chapter 3. At this stage a *caveat* (warning notice) could be raised, similarly as in the plenary procedure described above, which in this case was the method for preventing the granting of probate without the involvement of a creditor or other interested party - normally a relative of the deceased. Whilst some courts had a separate *Caveat Book* or *Caveat Register* the caveat was usually entered in the Court Act or Action Book as described below. If all was in order, the court officials *granted probate* (approved or proved the will), and the court decided what action should be taken; this was recorded in the *Probate Act* or *Action Book*, implying that the court had passed a Probate Act. This entry sometimes offers more details on the testator, his place of origin for example, than he gave in his will. In some courts the action was recorded on the back, or at the end, of the will, in some courts only in the Act Book and in other courts in both places. In some circumstances the probate could be limited to a particular portion of the estate - often the situation when the testator had property in England and Wales and also elsewhere; probate was then limited to dealing with only the English and Welsh property. Most such cases were proved in the Prerogative Court of Canterbury and recorded in separate *Limited Probate Books* otherwise the Probate Act Book was used. Sometimes, when part of an estate was in one ecclesiastical province, Limited Probate could be granted to cover the part in that province only. Probate was normally granted within a few weeks of a testator's death, but there are examples of Probate Acts being passed several years (up to 75 has been noted) later, waiting for a spouse to die or because of other complications.

On occasions a will had not been signed, or the signature of the testator had not been witnessed, or one of the witnesses or their spouses were beneficiaries of the estate. Each of these examples caused enormous complications, even rendering a will invalid. The 1837 Wills Act required a person to be over 21 when making a will for it to be valid. Prior to then any boy over 14 and any girl over 12 could make a will, though if the girl married her will became invalid if her husband did not agree to its provisions. Before 1883 [8.6] a will made by a married woman without the consent of her husband was invalid, although a will was valid if made by a widow (or a spinster). Not infrequently the parties involved, attending the ecclesiastical court, were so disappointed or disgusted on being told a will was invalid that they abandoned the document at the court when they left; in some cases these invalid wills were swept up by the court officials at the end of the day and were filed with the true records of the court, where they have remained to this day.

In the circumstances of an invalid will, or if no will could be located, the interested parties generally took steps for the court to grant them power to *administer* the estate of the deceased. In these situations *Administrators* were appointed by being granted *Letters of Administration* - abbreviated in the documents to *Admons.* Sometimes the executors of valid wills could not be located, having moved away or died, or they were under 21 years of age and so legally unable to act as executors, or once in a while the executors simply refused to undertake the required duties. In these cases the court appointed Administrators to act in place of the executors and they were granted *Letters-of-Administration-with-Will-Annexed.* Where the first-named executors renounced their rights in settling the estate the *Renunciations* were recorded in the court documents. In the Province of Canterbury, except in one or two areas (for example the City of London), the Church courts had no power to compel an Administrator to share out the remainder of the estate after paying the testator's debts and it was not unknown for him to keep it for his own use!

In some courts an executor was required to make a *Testamentary Bond* by which he undertook "well and truly to execute" the will, thereby providing evidence that a probate act or grant had been made, even if this was not recorded in the Act Book or on the will itself. At different periods of time some courts required an *Inventory* to be taken (often by a fellow-tradesman) of the personalty of the deceased to enable its full value to be calculated. Usually these inventories were filed with the wills.

After the will had been approved the original (or sometimes the copy) was officially sealed and given to the executor as evidence of probate and a copy (or sometimes the original) was filed with the Testamentary Court records. Filing is probably over-stating the reality of the situation as the wills were initially kept in bundles, rather haphazardly in many courts, although in some cases were later bound into books.

An additional opportunity, much encouraged in York, was available to the executor at this stage: he could have the will copied into yet another register of the testament-ary court. This entailed paying a fee for it to be entered into a volume of *Registered Wills*, but did not make it any more valid than an unregistered will, a copy of which was held by the court anyway. As many executors were unwilling to pay the fee more than a few wills remained unregistered, even though proved and quite valid.

It was necessary in some circumstances for testamentary courts to appoint guardians. If the minors were between 14 and 21 for boys or 12 and 21 for girls, *Curation Bonds* confirmed the appointment of *Curators*; for younger children, *Tuition Bonds*, appointing *Tutors*, were drawn up. The bonds were filed with the wills or Admin-istration Bonds. The appointments of curators and tutors were usually recorded in the Probate and Administration Act Books, although some courts kept separate Curation and Tuition Registers. *Orphan Books* were maintained by some courts and authorities; these books contain copies of wills of those testators who had left their children with no one to look after them.

If any interested parties believed that the executors or administrators were breaking their testamentary or administrative bonds, and not acting in accordance with the will or Letters of Administration, they could force an *Assignation* whereby fresh persons were appointed to well and truly administer the estate of the deceased. This could initiate a *Testamentary Suit* where the court moved from performing as a mere probate registry to having to settle disputes and pass judgments or pass sentences, as in plenary or summary cases. However, in a testamentary suit the first plea was called an *Allegation*, not a libel nor articles (see above). A few courts kept separate *Testamentary Sentence Registers*. Often the disputes were referred to a higher court, following the hierarchical structure outlined above; in such cases the higher court would issue a summons or citation in the form of a *Monition*, a *Commission*, or a *Requisition* to the lower court for copies of the relevant documentation (the lower court was admonished or commissioned to send up the documents). Normally the will was needed by the lower court in which case that court made a copy of it for their files and passed on the original. A note such as *"by decree"*, *"int dec"*, or *"by sentence"* was generally added to the will to indicate this had happened. In the Prerogative Court of Canterbury the whole of a testamentary suit was termed a sentence and was sometimes filed as such, i.e. under S in preference to the initial letter of the testator's surname.

9. Ecclesiastical Court Sentences

Depending on the findings of a typical ecclesiastical court, a judge, in pronouncing sentence at the conclusion of the hearing, might impose on either laity or clergy, a *monition*, a *penance, suspension ab ingressu ecclesiae* or *excommunication*, depending on the severity of the offence. On the clergy alone a judge might impose *suspension, sequestration, deprivation* or *degradation*. These sentences are discussed in the paragraphs below.

Heresy, denial of the essential doctrines of Christianity, was regarded as beyond reproach. Before the Reformation, Protestants were regarded as heretics, and afterwards initially some vociferous Catholics, Anabaptists (Unitarians) and other dissenters were also accused of promoting heretical doctrines. Witchcraft was treated by the Inquisition from 1258 as heresy and in 1484 Pope Innocent VIII issued a Bull in a determined effort to eradicate all witches. The punishment, based on Biblical laws in Exodus [9.1], was execution, generally by burning; in Britain, however, the Church tended to avoid pronouncing the death penalty, and merely excommunicated the guilty and then passed them to the temporal courts which took responsibility for any ultimate dispatch. English secular statutes of 1400, 1414 and 1539 certainly declared that heretics should be burned to death; the last heretic to be executed by burning in England was William Wightman (an Anabaptist) at Lichfield on 11 April 1612. In England such victims were usually first killed by strangulation and not burned alive.

Sentences on laity & clergy

The *monition*, sometimes termed an *admonition*, involved a mere reprimand and was the lightest form of ecclesiastical censure. A typical offence by a member of the laity which occasioned monition was to erect a tombstone without the permission of the incumbent of the parish.

Penance was regarded as being inflicted on the body of the person who was expected to feel penitent and could be either *public, private* or *solemn*. In fact a penance, although imposed as a sentence, was seen more as an expression of repentance by the guilty party than as a punishment. Cases of incest or incontinency (sexual offences) were usually punished by a penance.

Public penance, as intimated in Chapter 8, could be commuted at the discretion of a court by a Decree of Commutation of Penance for a monetary payment to a charity. The decree, which was signed by the judge, named the sum and the charity to which the commuted penance was to be paid (see Question 43 in the *Articles of Enquiry* in

Chapter 2). After the Reformation the public penance could involve attending divine service barelegged and bareheaded, clothed in a white sheet and holding a white rod. Convicted persons were required to publicly confess their sins during the service after the first lesson, and seek forgiveness from the congregation. In some cases the penance was performed in the market place instead of the church. The incumbent and the churchwardens had to subsequently report the successful completion of the penance to the court who had passed the sentence - thus leaving tangible evidence of its enactment. A *private penance* was performed before only the incumbent and the churchwardens of the penitent's parish.

Solemn penance, which was encouraged by Archbishop Peckham in the thirteenth century, was used originally for all sexual sins and could last continuously for two or more years, although later it was performed only during Lent for those two or more years. At the commencement of Lent the offender was formally turned out of the church by the bishop; on Maundy Thursday he was reconciled and absolved, and received the Sacrament on Easter Sunday. The final reconciliation had to be by a bishop although the reconciliation in the intervening years could be performed by an incumbent. A solemn penance should have been pronounced only once on an individual; if anyone later relapsed, the only action was for them to be thrust into a monastery or be disowned by the Church. In practice some people, habitual sexual offenders, performed a solemn penance on more than one occasion.

Suspension ab ingressu ecclesiae was a temporary withholding of some of the privileges of the Church; privileges included attending divine service, or receiving the sacrament. In practice suspension amounted to a temporary excommunication.

The heaviest spiritual sentence that could be imposed on both laity and clergy was *excommunication*. This would have been enacted by sending a Letter of Excommunication to the accused's parish for it to be read aloud during divine service at the parish church. A *contumacy* (failure to appear in answer to a threefold citation) was regarded as serious enough to be punishable by excommunication, as was persistent failure to perform a penance.

Strictly there were two sorts of excommunication, a *lesser* and a *greater*; the lesser, also referred to as an *interdict*, excluded the offender from attending divine service and receiving the sacrament, in other words it was a separation from passive communion, while the greater excommunication additionally excluded the offender from the company of all Christians. Prior to the Reformation there were very elaborate instructions on how the procedure should include certain rituals, such as the use of bell, book and candle, in the greater excommunication of heretics when the offenders were anathematised. This was based on the New Testament text "If any man love not the Lord Jesus Christ let him be anathema" [9.2]. The procedure involved the bishop pronouncing the malediction, closing his book (to symbolise removing the anathematised from the book of Christian life), throwing a lighted candle to the floor (extinguishing his soul from God as the light goes out before the congregation) and tolling a bell (as at a funeral). At some ceremonies the bishop was accompanied by twelve priests (to signify Christ and his apostles) also bearing lighted candles who all threw them to the ground.

Until 1813 [9.3] a person who was excommunicated additionally suffered civil disabilities such as being unable to serve on a jury, to be a witness in any court, to bring any action to recover property and may even have been imprisoned under a writ *de excommunicato capiendo* until reconciled to the Church. A *signification* could be sent from the ecclesiastical courts to the temporal courts seeking to capture the excommunicate, but it was rarely used. The civil disabilities were removed in 1813 and the only imprisonments liable (a maximum of six months) were those imposed by the ecclesiastical courts in their sentencing. Since 1641 [9.4] the church courts had not been permitted to impose fines, imprisonment or corporal punishment, although for those in holy orders the sentences of suspension, deprivation and deposition (see below) were, in practice, fines.

Sentences on clergy alone

On the clergy the judge could additionally impose, besides the above sentences, a more severe *suspension, deprivation* of an office or benefice, *deposition* or even *degradation*. Following degradation the cleric could be tried in a temporal court.

Suspension for the clergy - which often included a *sequestration* (impounding) of the clergyman's income or funds, from either office or benefice or both for a defined period of time - was imposed on a temporary basis, normally only after a previous admonition; if, however, the offence was particularly grave, suspension was immediate. Suspension could be imposed if, for example, a cleric was found guilty of keeping a fast other than appointed by statute; if he persisted he could be excommunicated or even deposed (see below). During the period of suspension the clergyman was not permitted to preach or undertake any clerical duties or to receive any profits from his benefice. A sequestrator was appointed by a bishop to receive the cleric's profits; during the sequestration the bishop, after 1871 [9.5], had the power to license and pay, at a fixed rate, a curate or curates to look after the parish during its continuance. The sequestration was regarded as being a civil process, although confusingly sequestration was sometimes used as a punishment for an ecclesiastical crime such as immorality, non-residence, or intemperate conduct.

Deprivation was the censure whereby a clergyman was permanently deprived of his office or benefice - in other words deprived of his spiritual dignity and living so that he was permanently denied access to any income from that benefice. This contrasts with suspension which was a temporary withdrawal of his benefits. Deprivation could be imposed only by an ecclesiastical judge in the presence, or with the agreement, of a bishop or archbishop - except in the Court of Arches or the Chancery Court of York where the Dean or the Auditor was each empowered to impose this sentence unaided. There were twenty-one causes allowed by common law (in other words bound by Statute) and eleven by canon law which could result in deprivation, some of which occasioned even greater censures; those under common law included not being ordained, illiteracy, not following the Book of Common Prayer, incontinence, drunkenness, and felling timber on church property unless for repairs. Causes under canon law which could occasion deprivation included wearing arms, simony (such as demanding money for sacraments) and non-residence of a rector.

Deposition was a stage further than deprivation as the clergyman was not only deprived of his office or benefice but he was also permanently inhibited from exercising his orders, though not deprived of them. This was little comfort as he could never again honestly earn a livelihood as a clergyman. A typical cause for deposition was keeping, on a third occasion, a fast other than appointed by statute - on the first occasion the clergyman was merely suspended (see above).

Degradation involved depriving a clergyman of his holy orders and degrading him to the laity. Canon 122 required that this sentence might be pronounced only by a bishop, assisted in his judgment by either his chancellor, dean and some of the prebendaries; or by an archdeacon and at least two grave ministers and preachers. Causes which might have resulted in degradation included disclosing confessions and keeping a concubine. Following degradation the cleric could be tried in a temporal court. The original reason for this process was to permit him to be tried for heresy and punished accordingly by a temporal court, usually by burning at the stake; this was not possible while he was in holy orders - he was protected from appearing in the temporal court by the benefit of clergy as described above and the ecclesiastical courts could not impose the death penalty.

Absolution

Absolution could be granted to suspended or excommunicated persons after their court appearances, or after they had successfully pleaded legitimate excuse and paid the fees of their contumacy.

10. Records of the Courts and their Officials

Available records

The wide range of documents generated by officials working in and for the various ecclesiastical courts, identified in Chapter 8, offers enormous scope for research. Originally held in provincial or diocesan, or in some cases unexpected, registries and archives, records of the ecclesiastical courts are in a variety of locations today. The present whereabouts of the original records, some transcribed, others abstracted, some translated and indexed, and some published, are identified in this chapter. You may find it beneficial to refer back to Chapter 8 for definitions and explanations of some of the terms employed here.

The most useful records of the ecclesiastical courts for biographers and for those studying migration patterns and movements of individuals, are the attestations or depositions in the summary procedures where the witnesses are often described in considerable depth. For example, a deponent (witness) may give his name, age, sex, condition, occupation, his length of residence in the place about which he is giving evidence, his present abode (if different) and, in some examples, all his previous abodes back to his birthplace.

On the other hand, for family historians the records of plenary procedures may provide a broader picture of the activities of individuals. Until 1733 most records were in Latin, although some depositions, *responsa personalia* and schedules of penances are in English. Appeal court records, such as those of the Court of Arches and of the Chancery Court of York, or of the High Court of Delegates and its successor the Judicial Committee of the Privy Council, typically contain similar information to that outlined above; in many examples these records include notes on the salient points of the causes in the lower courts from which they had been referred.

The large numbers of documents emanating from plenary proceedings for some courts were bound into volumes, variously in different archdeaconries and dioceses, and varying also as the times changed. For some courts similar series of documents: decrees, caveats, depositions and so on, for all cases, were bound into sequential or annual volumes; in other courts all the documents for each case were collected together. Some material has been indexed over the years to varying standards, but rarely can the names of all witnesses be found in most indexes, thus presenting the serious researcher with an interesting challenge.

Initiating procedures

Various procedures, such as drawing up a mailing list, issuing Articles of Enquiry, conducting a Visitation and issuing a citation, were essential to initiate an actual hearing of an ecclesiastical court. The Articles of Enquiry, such as quoted in Chapter 2, offer a useful understanding of subsequent court hearings. All the initiating procedures, described in some depth in Chapters 1 and 8, generated documents of varying quality. Nevertheless, these initiating records can prove as interesting as the records of the hearings themselves and should never be ignored. In some courts, the diverse documentation required to organise a Visitation are collectively termed Visitation Books, in others they are identified by their specific names, *liber cleri, liber actorum*, and so on. Today these books for the Province of Canterbury and its dioceses may be found in Lambeth Palace Library [10.1], the Public Record Office [10.2], the National Library of Wales [10.3] or diocesan archives, mostly now in county record offices [10.4]. For the Province of York and its dioceses similar records are in the Borthwick Institute of Historical Research of the University of York [10.5] or diocesan archives or county record offices. Many of the initiating records are easily read these days, having been transcribed, indexed and published; for example, *Visitations in Lincoln Diocese* by the Lincoln Record Society [10.6] and those in Buckingham Archdeaconry by the Buckinghamshire Record Society [10.7]. Examples for the northern province include activities of the Archbishops of York in various volumes in the *Yorkshire Archaeological Society Record Series* [10.8] and the *Texts and Calendars* series of the Borthwick Institute [10.9].

Business in all courts

A registrar recorded the business conducted at a court hearing, normally soon after the business was completed, although long afterwards in some cases. A description of the hearing, including that of a correctional case following a Visitation, was entered into an Act Book or Court Book; but on some occasions, especially instance cases, the account was extremely brief and gave only the names of the parties, and not even the charge against the defendant. Some descriptions are simply abbreviated notes with as many as four cases recorded on one page. In fact, it appears that in some courts the registrar pragmatically allocated four cases to a page, irrespective of the court business, and then he was forced to use cramped writing and incongruous abbreviations to record the hearing. The Cause Papers, if they survive, are often more useful than the Act Books (but for probate business see below), although in the late fifteenth and early sixteenth centuries the clerks sometimes included the evidence of witnesses in the Act Books.

Office cases not only had their proceedings logged in the Act Book, but also often required other documents to be drawn up, as described in Chapter 8; some of these documents have survived including letters of proxy with substitution clauses, citations, schedules of penance or confession, and decrees of commutation of penance. A Corrections Book was used by some courts to record the deliberations of office cases rather than the Act Book. At some periods in the smaller dioceses, one book was used to register all summary and plenary correction cases and probate records. Process Books in the appeal courts were used to enter copies of the *materia* (processes or detailed reports of the cases) first heard in a lower court.

Drafts

In some ecclesiastical courts a draft record of the case was made before being entered into the formal Act Book and some of these drafts have survived: the Court of Arches, for example, has Acts of Court from 1679 to 1818 as rough drafts as well as the Act Books mentioned below. A few disparate Draft Acts for the Prerogative Court of Canterbury from 1666 to 1857 have also survived and are in the same repositories (see in the Prerogative courts section below) as the formal records. Such drafts can prove invaluable if the formal Act or Court Books are missing.

Archdeacons' courts

So many cases in the Archdeacons' Courts concerned incontinency (adultery and fornication) that the courts became known as "Bawdy Courts"; the cases arose largely from presentments which had been made during the archdeacons' regular visitations. A comprehensive overview of the work of these courts, with references from all over the country, was presented in 1943 by E R C Brinkworth - although his survey was somewhat misleadingly entitled "from Oxford Records 1566 to 1759" [10.10]. Some very detailed studies of court records have been undertaken for various archdeaconries, noteworthy among which is that by F G Emmison [10.11] on Essex material for the first Elizabethan period. A lighter look (but which is academically referenced) at published material, primarily from archdeacons' courts but from other courts as well, was edited by Paul Hair [10.12]. Both of these works illustrate the enormous range of cases with which archdeacons were confronted. For the present whereabouts of records of archdeacons' courts, see the next section.

Bishops' (Episcopal) courts

David M Smith undertook a survey of bishops' registers from the Middle Ages to 1646 [10.13], indicating their whereabouts in 1981. However, most (but see below) of the diocesan registries have been closed and generally appropriate county archivists have been appointed as custodians of those archives. Thus the Act Books and other records of the archdeacons' and the bishops' courts, and of many peculiar courts, for both disputed and simple licensing causes, are likely to be in county record offices nowadays. Notable exceptions are the records of the dioceses of Canterbury and York which were, as described in Chapter 4, presided over by the archbishops of Canterbury and York respectively. Whilst the York diocesan records and those of other courts (Exchequer and Chancery, for example) for which the Archbishop of York had a nominal responsibility, are, not unexpectedly, with his records in the Borthwick Institute, most of those for Canterbury diocese are with the Canterbury Commissary archives in Canterbury Cathedral Library [10.14]. Other Canterbury diocesan records, such as the mediaeval bishops' registers, are in Lambeth Palace Library. Other exceptions where diocesan archives are not in county record offices are those for all Welsh dioceses at the National Library of Wales.

Prerogative courts

For the Prerogative Court of Canterbury (PCC), besides the books of Draft Acts identified above, other surviving probate records include wills, both contemporary court copies and some originals, inventories, Act and Muniment Books, warrants, allegations, proxies, depositions, answers, sentences, exhibits, orders, caveat books, bonds, proctors' case papers, processes, and bills of taxed costs. The probate records of the PCC from 1384 to 1858 are held at the Public Record Office. The Probate Act Books, which run almost continuously from 1526, are certainly worth consulting as in many cases they contain additional information on testators not found in the wills themselves (see Chapter 8). The wills, in groups of years, and some Act Books and Sentences, have been largely indexed and the results published over many years by the British Record Society and a variety of other organisations and individuals. These publications are identified in J S W Gibson's *Probate Jurisdictions* [10.15].

A similar series of probate records has survived for the Prerogative Court of York (PCY) from 1591 and may be located at the Borthwick Institute, though only from 1624 are they in separate Act Books. Prior to 1624 most PCY wills were entered into the York City Act Books. As the PCY operated in conjunction with other courts in the Province of York (see Chapter 4), many of its documents are filed with those of the Exchequer Court of York, and with those of the Chancery Court of York, and a few with those of the York Consistory Court. There are no published indexes to purely PCY probate records and whilst the wills and administrations from 1316 to 1822, edited by J Charlesworth and A V Hudson and published in 1937 by the Yorkshire Archaeological Society [10.16], are enticingly termed "Archbishops' Registers", they are entirely of probate granted in the Chancery Court of York. The Yorkshire Archaeological Society has, however, published indexes of a great deal of probate material granted before 1688 [10.17] and there are manuscript indexes of later material at the Borthwick Institute. A J Camp's *Wills and Their Whereabouts* [10.18] elaborates on the complexities of PCY jurisdiction and its resultant records, although some fresh information has come to light since that publication.

In the absence of a will, admons granted by the PCC or the PCY, or more accurately the registered entry of grants and the bonds, are in either the Public Record Office or the Borthwick Institute, as are any associated inventories and also the enormous amount of documentation created by the courts arising from disputed probate cases. Many indexes and other finding aids for this PCC and PCY material have been published by the bodies identified above, and there are unpublished indexes at those major archives. Probate records for the Interregnum period (1653 to 1660) granted by civil judges throughout most of the country have now been added to the PCC series in the Public Record Office.

Audience courts

Separate Audience Courts records have not survived in vast numbers. Any surviving records of the Court of Audience for the Province of Canterbury prior to 1660 are with those of the Court of Arches (see below) with which it was merged in that year, although almost all of these pre-1660 records were destroyed in the Fire of London. The Court of Audience records for York Province are in the Borthwick Institute; (see Chapter 4 for details on the relationship of this court with others in this province). There is some evidence of Audience cases in the 1306-15 register of Archbishop William Greenfield, published by the Surtees Society from 1931 to 1940.

A thorough analysis of the cases brought before the Salisbury Audience Court between 1315 and 1329 was presented by Mrs Dorothy Owen at the Cambridge Legal History Conference in July 1975 [10.19], even though this Audience Court Act Book was not particularly well identified among the other registers of Bishop Roger Martival of Salisbury. Audience Court records for other dioceses have been transcribed and published, some with most useful introductions. Interesting examples are the work of Mrs Margaret Bowker for the Lincoln Audience Court from 1514 to 1520 [10.20], that of Charles Johnson for Rochester Audience Court from 1321 to 1330 [10.21] - but not identified as such - and that of Dr R M Haines for a 1349 Worcester Audience Court [10.22]. Several other Audience Court records are mixed with those for other episcopal courts - see Dorothy Owen's analysis.

Convocations

Original Convocation records are formally open for inspection only by members of Convocation, unless by special leave; in practice today serious students are able to study the records at Lambeth Palace Library or the Borthwick Institute - see below. The dates of meetings of Convocations and other Councils, held in Canterbury, York and elsewhere from the years 602 to 1536, are identified in the *Handbook of British Chronology*, second edition edited by Sir F M Powicke and E B Fryde, published by the Royal Historical Society in 1961. It may be noted that from 1717 until 1852 in

Canterbury and from 1698 to 1861 in York, Convocations were suspended because of the political wrangling of Whig bishops and Tory clergy.

The Canterbury Provincial Convocation records were at one stage stored at Doctors' Commons. At the beginning of the eighteenth century they were moved from "the dust and cobwebs" (to quote Archbishop Tenison who died in 1715) to Lambeth Palace. The original records prior to 1640 appear to have perished but, as mentioned in Chapter 1, Wilkins transcribed the majority of them and included them in his *Concilia* in 1737, and so they are obviously accessible wherever copies of that publication are held. From 1640 the original documents are extant. A somewhat dated, but nonetheless interesting, article by J Armitage Robinson on the early history and records of the Canterbury Convocation was published in 1915 [10.23].

The records of Convocation of the Province of York from 1460 to 1950, in 143 boxes of chronologically arranged documents, and from 1545 to 1928 in sixteen Convocation Books, are in the Borthwick Institute. Detail on the records of this court and their content from 1279 to 1714 are in G W Kitchin's *Records of the Northern Convocation*, published in 1907 by the Surtees Society [10.24]. The Minutes and Acts of the York Provincial Convocation from 1859 to 1964 have been published in the 40 volumes of the *York Journal of Convocation*; copies are at the Borthwick Institute and at Lambeth Palace Library.

Records of the Church Assembly and the General Synod (see page 78) are kept at Church House, Westminster, London [10.25].

Heresy courts

The records of the Courts for the Trial of Heresy, which were sometimes entered in the archbishops' registers, and the records of the Courts for the Trial of Bishops in the Provinces for Canterbury and York are respectively in Lambeth Palace Library and the Borthwick Institute, although there is little evidence that the York heresy court ever met.

Court of Arches & Chancery Court of York

As outlined in Chapters 3 and 4, decisions made in the archbishops' courts could be referred to a higher court. In the Province of Canterbury, the immediate appellate court was the Court of Arches, whereas in the Province of York immediate appeal was to either the Consistory or the Chancery Court of York until the late seventeenth century, and thereafter to solely this Chancery Court.

Some interesting articles by Dorothy Slatter on the Court of Arches and its records, now held in Lambeth Palace Library, were published in 1953 and 1955 [10.26]. The court records include decrees, appeals, papers exhibited, Act Books from 1635 to 1636 and 1660 to 1773, Acts of Court, Process Books, case papers and books relating to proctors. There are separate Sentences volumes from 1560 to 1561, 1622 to 1640 and 1661 to 1797. Unfortunately, as mentioned above, most of the earlier records of this court, with those of the Canterbury Audience Court, were lost in the Fire of London in 1666; even from 1660 the documents are in rather a poor state, having been stored in a well in St Paul's Churchyard at one stage. An extremely useful index of the cases from 1660 to 1913 has been published by the British Record Society [10.27].

Because the role of the Chancery Court of York was by no means as clear-cut as that of the Court of Arches, as explained in Chapter 4, its records are less easily codified and most are found with Exchequer Court material at the Borthwick Institute. The probate documents of the York Chancery Court include wills, admons and inventories from 1535 to 1857. The Chancery Act Books exist from 1525 to 1943, though with some gaps. The probate records of the York Consistory Court (also used for appeals) have been mentioned in the Prerogative court section above. Some indexes have been published by the Yorkshire Archaeological Society.

Papal court
Prior to the Reformation, appeals from the Court of Arches, or from the York Chancery Court, could be made to the Papal Court. Some of the records of the Papal Court convened in the British Isles and of the Court of Papal Court Delegates prior to the Reformation are in the Department of Manuscripts at the British Library [10.28], although there are some Papal Bulls and Letters in the Public Record Office and others are in Lambeth Palace Library. A *Calendar of Papal Letters* [in the Public Record Office] *relating to the British Isles* for the period from 1198 to 1492 was published between 1893 and 1960 in fourteen volumes, with several abstracted portions translated into English. After 1960 the Irish Manuscripts Commission took responsibility for publishing later years of these Papal documents, and issued their first volume in 1978. A survey of Papal documents in Lambeth Palace Library, in the form of a catalogue with translated extracts and summaries by Professor Jane Sayers, was published in 1967 [10.29]. Her book *Papal Judges Delegate in the Province of Canterbury, 1198 to 1254* has already been alluded to [10.30]. The 1959 book by Robert Brentano [10.31] on Papal Judges Delegate in the Province of York during the late thirteenth century merits a greater readership.

High Court of Delegates
Following the Reformation, as explained in Chapter 3, ecclesiastical court appeals could no longer be made to a Papal Court and temporal appellate courts were opened. For the High Court of Delegates the Act Books run from 1538 to 1700 in a bound series and then continue to 1758; these records are now in the Public Record Office [10.32], having been in a variety of repositories over the past 150 years.

Depositions of witnesses from 1564 to 1685 are bound, but continue to 1735 whereas the answers run from 1655 to 1711. The sentences are from 1585 to 1802 while the Muniment Books, which contain mostly appeals against probate, run from 1652 to 1859 and are very usefully indexed, as are the Assignation Books in bound volumes from 1650 to 1838, and the Case Books from 1796 to 1834. However, the Cause Papers (1600 to 1834), the Process Papers (1609 to 1834), and the wills and affidavits (1662 to 1857) are not indexed within the documents themselves; but an index to 550 wills and admons from 1651 to 1857 which came before this court was published in volumes 11 and 12 of *The Genealogist* in 1887/8. There are also many miscellaneous records such as accounts, bills and interlocutions from 1660 to 1833, and some records which refer to Privy Council appeals, running even to 1866. You should be aware that the High Court of Delegates not only served as the appeal court from the ecclesiastical courts, but also as the final appellate from the High Court of Admiralty, the Court of Chivalry and the Courts of the Chancellors of the Universities (Oxford and Cambridge). Thus when researching Delegates court records you will discover many cases unrelated to ecclesiastical matters or even unrelated to the secular aspects of the work of the church courts.

Some of the fees occasioned in the High Court of Delegates from 1811, which were noted in the High Court of Admiralty records, appear in the Accounts Books of the Instance and Prize Courts of the High Court of Admiralty; these are now in the Public Record Office [10.33]. In the same series are the Minutes Books of Appeals (1866 to 1948) of the High Court of Admiralty.

Judicial Committee of the Privy Council
For the Judicial Committee of the Privy Council there are, in the Public Record Office [10.34], seventeen volumes of Assignation Books (1833 to 1878), Case Books (1834 to 1870) and 566 volumes and bundles of Process Papers (1834 to 1879) which are a direct continuation of the High Court of Delegates series. There are also some miscellaneous records including instruments, judgments and bills of costs which run from 1833 to 1865, and other voluminous records of the Committee, including the Appeals Process Papers, Assignation and Case Books and miscellaneous documents. Some references to ecclesiastical court appeals to the Committee from 1866 to 1876 appear in the Minutes Books of Appeals (1866 to 1948) in the High Court of Admiralty. A useful table of the names of all the members of the Committee from 1833 to 1876 and which meetings they attended is given by Howell in the Appendix to his book [10.35] on the Committee.

Courts of High Commission
The records of the Court of High Commission for Ecclesiastical Causes in the Province of Canterbury were ordered, by Parliament, to be destroyed during the

Civil War; however, the Minutes Books from 18 February 1634 to 7 December 1640, with some gaps, escaped destruction and may be found among the State Papers Domestic for Charles I, now in the Public Record Office [10.36]. A few of the gaps for the remainder of the period during which this court was in operation (at least 1559 to 1640) can be filled by other documents such as sentences and writs that are scattered among the State Papers. Some of these dispersed items have been identified by Usher [10.37] in the bibliography to his book on this court; Usher's book also provides an alphabetical list of names of the Commissioners for Ecclesiastical Causes in the Province of Canterbury from 1549 to 1641. For the Province of York [10.38] the records of its Court of High Commission did not suffer the same fate and those Act Books run from 27 February 1562 to 28 April 1641 and there are very many Cause Papers, now in the Borthwick Institute [10.39]. Reports of cases in York from 20 October 1631 to 21 June 1632 were indexed and published by the Camden Society in 1886 [10.40].

There were also several diocesan High Commission Courts whose records have survived: those for Chester from 1562, for Norwich from 1595, for Winchester from 1606 and for Durham from 1626, to quote only four examples. Some of these have been transcribed, translated, edited and published by historical record societies or similar organisations; for example, for the Durham Diocesan Court of High Commission the contents of the Act Books (1628 to 1639) and the Depositions (1626 to 1638) have been made available by the Surtees Society [10.41]. Similar High Commission documents for other courts are in county record offices and have been published by various groups.

Non-judicial business

For the non-judicial administrative activities of an ecclesiastical court, such as app-roving faculties, issuing marriage licences, granting probate, recording inventories, and issuing miscellaneous licences for preachers, curates, schoolmasters, surgeons, midwives and Dissenting Meeting Houses, volumes quite separate from the judicial Corrections, Act or Court Books, many already identified in this chapter, were usually used to record the business. Some courts kept a separate record of the fees collected by the judge and by the registrar when licences were issued. However, it is obvious, by looking [10.42] at the records, that many courts charged quite different amounts from those laid down by statute (see Chapter 2).

A faculty to alter the fabric of a church may not be considered by a biographer or family historian to be worthy of inspection. But, appreciating that an alteration may have involved moving the pews - which were all allocated to named individuals and families - and the faculty included annotated plans of who sat where before and after the work, then biographical interest can be immense.

References to a great deal of the courts' non-judicial business may be found in Episcopal (Bishops') Registers, many of which have been published, for example by the Selden Society, the Canterbury and York Society, the Surtees Society, and the Yorkshire Archaeological Society. David Smith's 1981 survey on Bishops' Registers, mentioned above, gives a very useful indication of what is available. But bear in mind that these registers also contain information on activities outside the ecclesiastical courts - the more obvious very personal ceremonies, at which an archbishop ordained or instituted clergymen, were regarded as Acts of Ordination or Institution; accordingly details of such clergy were recorded in registers termed Institution Act Books.

After the Reformation the Master of Faculties in the Province of Canterbury was the issuing officer for the Archbishop of Canterbury for most non-contentious "licences, dispensations, compositions, faculties, grants, rescripts, delegacies, instruments and other writings", as mentioned in Chapter 3. When the Faculty Office began its work in April 1534 all dispensations were recorded in the same Muniment Books. Thus jumbled into the same record are details on dispensations for non-residence of clergymen, permission to hold benefices in plurality, ordination of clerics who were illegitimate, faculties to alter church buildings, issuing of marriage licences, conferring of honorary degrees and appointing notaries public. Over the years these dispensations and faculties and licences came to be recorded into separate registers.

The Faculty Office records are in Lambeth Palace Library, although many abstracts of Muniment Books and Registers have been published by various individuals and bodies. For example, a calendar of the registers from 1534 to 1549 with an explanatory introduction and index by D S Chambers, was published in 1966 [10.43]. The names of recipients of honorary, Lambeth, degrees with the dates on which they were conferred by the Archbishops of Canterbury from 1539 until 1864 were indexed and published in the *Gentleman's Magazine* for 1864 [10.44].

Estate Duty Office

Do not overlook that the secular Estate Duty Office used wills and Letters of Administration as indicators of potential sources of duty for government coffers, and in so doing maintained its own records. Although these are not ecclesiastical court records, a note about them is not inappropriate here, as they were associated with probate material, and very usefully assembled in an ordered fashion. However, a strict alphabetically arranged index, as found in a telephone directory, was not used, and the documents were calendared, in other words filed under the initial letter of the surname. The calendars of wills and admons compiled by the Inland Revenue department for the whole of England and Wales for the periods 1796 to 1811 and 1812 to 1857 are available to researchers at the PRO [10.45] in the Inland Revenue series of documents. For the first period the calendars are arranged by the initial letter of the surname plus the next vowel of the surname. For the second period the wills and admons are filed in blocks of the first three letters of the surname. Within the 1796 to 1811 period the calendars are in three groups: wills from the Prerogative Court of Canterbury (PCC), "alphabetically" by year and month when the Probate Act was passed; admons from the PCC "alphabetically" and roughly chrono-logically; wills and admons from the Prerogative Court of York (PCY) and all other probate courts, known collectively by the Inland Revenue as being from the "County Courts". Within the 1812 to 1857 period the calendars are in two groups: wills for all probate courts in England and Wales in annual volumes of four alphabetical parts; admons, divided into those granted in the PCC and those granted in the "County Courts".

Doctors' Commons

Doctors' Commons, being originally a club or society for Doctors of law, maintained a series of records of its members, as would any similar group or organisation. Unfortunately many of the records have been lost, but those that survive are full of names and brief biographical details of individuals - just the information that a biographer, genealogist or family historian seeks. The Subscription Book contains the names and signatures of most members living between 1511 and 1855, in the approximate order of their seniority of membership of the Society; this book also has their rules, copies of other important documents relating to their organisation, and some minutes of their early meetings. A list of thirty-eight advocates of the Court of Arches in 1576, of whom only fifteen were in practice, has survived among the State Papers for Elizabeth I. Although this is not strictly a Doctors' Commons' archive, it is a record of some early members of the Society.

The Doctors' Commons' Long Book is a term-by-term record of residential (those in commons) and non-residential members making various payments. Their Stewards and Treasurers also used this book for some of their accounts, and some inventories and copies of charters were recorded in it; from 1679 to 1828 the book was also used to record minutes of members' meetings. The Minutes Book proper contains minutes of meetings from 1828 to when the members met last on 10 July 1865. Whilst the Treasurers' Accounts Books from 1679 to 1730, from 1767 to 1838, and from 1839 to 1865 were more correct volumes than the Long Book, in which to record the Society's finances, they contain only summaries of payments. The Commons Book, which sadly runs only from 1738 until 1779, holds the names of the residential members but fascinatingly tells us how much wine they drank; and there are bundles of vouchers which run from 1708 until 1841, though with some gaps. The Rent Book gives names of tenants from 1787 to 1830 and indicates their payments for land tax, insurance and tithes. The Judges' and Advocates' Term Fees

Books provide a termly record of fees paid to servants, some named, and of payments for wine, food and land tax from 1768 to 1864. Similar records exist for the proctors from 1761 to 1858: the Proctors' Term Fees Books contain the names of all proctors practising in the Court of Arches and the contributions that they made, as fees, towards the repairs and other expenses of the court room. The Librarian's Account Book includes titles of books purchased for the Society library between 1736 and 1843. There is another record, very confusingly called an Income Book, which is actually an account of the money spent between 1730 and 1752 by each incoming tenant on repairs, and which was to be repaid by a succeeding tenant over the ensuing twenty years.

Most of the surviving records of Doctors' Commons are in Lambeth Palace Library [10.46]; however, the Long Book (also termed the Treasurer's Book) and the Librarian's Account Book are in the Public Record Office [10.47], the Charter is in All Souls College, Oxford [10.48], and the 1576 list of the advocates of the Court of Arches then living in London can be found among the State Papers, Domestic, in the Public Record Office [10.49]. The names of Advocates who were authorised by the Archbishop of Canterbury may be found in a card index at the Public Record Office.

Media reports

From the time when newspapers, periodicals and journals began to publish social events (as opposed to political or financial intelligence), reports of findings of ecclesiastical courts, both non-judicial and judicial, began to appear, though not nearly in such profusion as for the temporal courts. Reports on the causes themselves began in the mid-eighteenth century for the Prerogative Court of Canterbury and the Consistory Court of London, and gradually reports appeared of causes in other ecclesiastical courts. Some causes attracted greater coverage than others, but local and national newspapers and lawyers' journals, such as *Justice of the Peace*, are secondary records of the ecclesiastical courts that should not be overlooked. Many county record offices hold copies of the newspapers for their areas, often on microfilm or microfiche, and many local public libraries also have copies of local periodicals and papers. The British Library Newspaper Collection in north London [10.50] has many newspapers, periodicals and journals published locally and nationally throughout the British Isles.

Notes, References & Addresses

1.1. William Lyndwood. *Provinciale, seu Constitutiones Angliae; cum summariis....* London. 1432.
1.2. David Wilkins. *Concilia Magna Britanniae et Hiberniae....*1737; for more detail on this work, see in reference 1.15.
1.3. 25 Hen VIII, c.19 (1533).
1.4. 1 & 2 Philip & Mary, c.8 (1554).
1.5. 1 Eliz I, c.1 (1559).
1.6. 25 Hen VIII, c.19, s.7 (1533).
1.7. 13 & 14 Car II, c.4 (1662).
1.8. 13 Eliz I, c.12 (1571).
1.9. 28 & 29 Vic, c.12 (1865).
1.10. Richard Burn. *Ecclesiastical Law*. 9th edn. 1842. Vol 1, p xi.
1.11. Victor A Hatley. *The Church in Victorian Northampton*. Northants Record Society. Vol 37. 1992
1.12. Acts. ch 5. vv 1-11.
1.13. I Corinthians. ch 5. vv 1-5.
1.14. Colin R Chapman. *Growth of British Education and its Records*. Lochin Publishing. Reprint 1996.
1.15. Colin R Chapman. *Marriage Laws, Rites, Records & Customs*. Lochin Publishing. 1996.
1.16. On 8 April 1653.
1.17. [Commission on Ecclesiastical Courts]. *The Ecclesiastical Courts, Principles of Reconstruction*. SPCK. 1954.

2.1. The quoted text is as given in the 1741 publication, including contemporary spelling and the use of upper case and italic characters, although the questions were given Roman numerals in the original.
2.2. see 1.15 above.
2.3. 18 Eliz I, c.7 (1576).
2.4. 7 & 8 Geo IV, c.28 (1827).
2.5. 23 & 24 Vic, c.32 (1860).
2.6. 18 & 19 Vic, c.41 (1855).
2.7. 4 Geo IV, c.76 (1823).
2.8. 6 & 7 Wm IV, c.71 (1836).
2.9. 31 & 32 Vic, c.109 (1868).
2.10 3 & 4 Vic, c.86 (1840).
2.11. 1 & 2 Vic, c.106 (1838).
2.12. 61 & 62 Vic, c.48 (1898).
2.13. 3 Hen VIII, c.11 (1511).

3.1. 24 Hen VIII, c.12 (1533).
3.2. 25 Hen VIII, c.19 (1533).

3.3.   G I O Duncan. *High Court of Delegates.* Cambridge University Press. 1971.

3.4.   2 & 3 Wm IV, c.92 (1832).

3.5.   3 & 4 Wm IV, c.41 (1833).

3.6.   20 & 21 Vic, c.77 (1858).

3.7.   J E Sayers. *Papal Judges Delegate in the Province of Canterbury 1198-1254.* OUP. 1971.

3.8.   23 Hen VIII, c.9 (1531).

3.9.   R G Usher. *Rise and Fall of the High Commission.* Clarendon Press, Oxford. 1913. See also: J S Burn. *The High Commission.* 1865.

3.10.   Samuel R Gardiner. *Reports of Cases....* Camden Society. New series. Vol 39. 1886, pp 181-322.

3.11.   P Tyler. In a new Introduction to R G Usher [see 3.9]. 1968.

3.12.   Richard M Wunderli. *London Church Courts....* Medieval Academy of America. 1981.

3.13.   25 Hen VIII, c.21 (1533).

3.14.   21 & 22 Vic, c.90 (1858).

3.15.   Based on the settling by Lanfranc of a dispute between the two archbishops in 1072. *Rolls series* pp 63-65. It was in 1353 that the Archbishop of Canterbury became styled "Primate of All England" with the Archbishop of York "Primate of England".

3.16.   20 & 21 Vic, c.77 (1857).

3.17.   20 & 21 Vic, c.85 (1857).

3.18.   [Royal Commission on Ecclesiastical Courts]. *General Report.* 15 Feb 1832.

3.19.   58 Geo III, c.45 (1818).

4.1.   An early province of Caerleon in Wales was subsumed into Canterbury during Henry I's reign.

4.2.   T Lathbury. *A History of the Convocation of the Church of England to 1742.* London. 2nd edn. 1853. [1st edn was 1842].

4.3.   R R Pearce. *Law Relating to Convocation of the Clergy with Forms of Proceedings in the Provinces of Canterbury and York.* 1848.

5.1.   According to a Bull of Pope Boniface VIII in 1300.

5.2.   25 Hen VIII, c.21 (1533).

5.3.   37 & 38 Vic, c.85 (1874).

5.4.   38 & 39 Vic, c.76 (1875).

5.5.   Edmund Gibson. *Codex juris ecclesiastici Anglicani: or the statutes, constitutions, canons, rubrics and articles of the Church of England, methodically digested under their proper heads; with a commentary historical and judicial....* London. 1713. p xxvi.   [The second edition, in English, was published 1761.]

5.6.   37 Hen VIII, c.17 (1545).

5.7.   Enacted by the clergy in Convocation - Canon 127 specifically.

6.1.   40 & 41 Vic, c.25 (1877).

6.2.   Ronald A Marchant. *The Church under the Law.* Cambridge University Press. 1969, p 32.

6.3.   William Lyndwood. Op cit. p 235.

6.4.   Canon 38 of the Fourth Lateran Council.

7.1.   Colin R Chapman. *How Heavy, How Much & How Long?* Lochin Publishing. 1995, repr. 1996.

7.2.   G D Squibb. *Doctors' Commons.* Clarendon Press. Oxford. 1977.

7.3.   Henry Hickman, son of Sir Anthony of Woodford, Essex, MP for Northampton 1601; will proved 4
       Sep 1618 at Westminster.

7.4.   6 & 7 Wm IV, c.77 (1836).

7.5.   20 & 21 Vic, c.77 (1857).

7.6.   21 & 22 Vic, c.95 (1858).

7.7.   20 & 21 Vic, c.85 (1857).

7.8.   22 & 23 Vic, c.6 (1859).

7.9.   3 & 4 Vic, c.85 (1840).

7.10. 36 & 37 Vic, c.66 (1871).

8.1.   16 Car I, c.11 (1641).

8.2.   13 Car II, st 1, c.12 (1661).

8.3.   17 & 18 Vic, c.47 (1854).

8.4.   32 Hen VIII, c.1 (1540).

8.5.   7 Will IV & 1 Vic, c.26 (1837).

8.6.   45 & 46 Vic, c.75 (1883).

9.1.   Exodus. ch 22. v 18.

9.2.   I Corinthians. ch 16. v 22.

9.3.   53 Geo III, c.127 (1813).

9.4.   16 Car I, c.11 (1641).

9.5.   34 & 35 Vic, c. 45 (1871).

10.1.   Lambeth Palace Library, London SE1 7JU.

10.2.   Public Record Office, Ruskin Avenue, Kew TW9 4DU.

10.3.   National Library of Wales, Aberystwyth, Dyfed SY23 3BU.

10.4.   Jeremy.Gibson & Pamela Peskett. *Record Offices: How to Find Them.* Fed of Fam Hist Socs. 1996

10.5.   University of York, Borthwick Institute of Historical Research, Peasholme Grn, York YO1 2PW.

10.6.   A Hamilton Thompson. *Visitations in the Diocese of Lincoln.* Lincoln Rec Society. Vol 33. 1940.

10.7.   E R C Brinkworth. *Episcopal Visitation Book.* Buckinghamshire Record Society. Vol 7. 1947.

10.8.   For example: S L Ollard (ed). *Archbishop Herring's Visitation Returns, 1743.* Yorkshire
        Archaeological Society, Record Series. Vols 71, 72, 75, 77, 79. 1928-31.

10.9.   For example: W J Sheils. *Archbishop Grindal's Visitation of the Diocese of York, 1575*;
        and: *Borthwick Texts and Calendars.* No 4. 1977.

10.10. E R C Brinkworth. *Transactions, Royal Historical Society.* 4th Series. Vol 25. 1943.

10.11. F G Emmison. *Elizabethan Life: Morals & the Church Courts.* Essex Record Office. 1973.

10.12. P Hair. *Before the Bawdy Court.* Elek. 1972.

10.13. David M Smith. *Guide to the Bishops' Registers of England and Wales.* Royal Hist Soc. 1981.

10.14. Canterbury Cathedral Archives and Library, The Precincts, Canterbury CT1 2EG.

10.15. Jeremy Gibson. *Probate Jurisdictions, Where to Look for Wills*. FFHS. 1994.

10.16. J Charlesworth. *Wills and Administrations in the Registers of Archbishops of York, 1316-1822.* YASRS. Vol 93. 1937; see also YASRS. Vol 73. 1928.

10.17. For example, YASRS. Vols 4, 6, 11, 14, 19, 22, 24, 26, 28, 32, 35, 49, 60, 68, 89. 1888-1934.

10.18. A J Camp. *Wills and their Whereabouts*. Phillimore & Co. 1963.

10.19. This was subsequently published: D M Owen. *An Episcopal Audience Court* in: *Legal Records and the Historian*. Royal Historical Society. 1978.

10.20. Margaret Bowker. *An Episcopal Court Book 1514-20*. Lincoln Record Society. Vol 61. 1967.

10.21. Charles Johnson. *Hamonis Hethe 1319-52*. Canterbury & York Soc. Vols 48 & 49. 1948 & 1949.

10.22. R M Haines. *Register of Wolstan de Bransford 1339-49*. Worcester Hist Society. Vol 4. 1966.

10.23. J A Robinson. *Canterbury Convocation Records*. Church Quarterly Review. Oct 1915, pp 81-137.

10.24. G W Kitchin. *The Records of the Northern Convocation*. Surtees Society. Vol 113. 1907.

10.25. General Synod Office, Church House, Great Smith Street, London SW1P 3NZ.

10.26. D M Slatter, *Journal of Ecclesiastical History*. Vol IV, Oct 1953, pp 139-153; and *Journal of the Society of Archivists*. Vol 1 No 2. April 1955, pp 29-31.

10.27. British Record Society. *Index Library*. Vol 85. 1972.

10.28. British Library, 96 Euston Road, St Pancras, London NW1 2DB.

10.29. J E Sayers. *Original Papal Documents in Lambeth Palace Library*. Athlone Press. 1967.

10.30. J E Sayers. *Papal Judges Delegate in the Province of Canterbury, 1195-1254*. OUP. 1971.

10.31. R Brentano. *York Metropolitan Jurisdiction and Papal Judges Delegate, 1279-1296*. University of California Publications in History. Vol 58. 1959.

10.32. See 10.2. above; in series DEL 1 to 11.

10.33. See 10.2. above; in series HCA 2 and 60.

10.34. See 10.2. above; in series PCAP 1, 2, 3, and 5.

10.35. P A Howell. *Judicial Committee of the Privy Council, 1833-1876*. Cambridge Univ. Press. 1979.

10.36. See 10.2. above; in series SP16.

10.37. See 3.9. above.

10.38. Usher's work (see 3.9 above) was reprinted in 1968 with a new introduction by Philip Tyler who referenced York provincial and other diocesan material that was unknown to Usher.

10.39. See 10.5. above; in series HC 1 to 19.

10.40. Samuel R Gardiner. *Reports of Cases....* Camden Society. New series. Vol 39. 1886, pp 181-322.

10.41. W H D Longstaff. *Acts of High Commission Court within Durham*. Surtees Society. Vol 34. 1858.

10.42. R A Marchant. Op.cit. pp 24-30.

10.43. D S Chambers. *A Calendar of Faculty Office Registers 1534-1549*. Clarendon Press. 1966.

10.44. *Gentleman's Magazine*. New series. Vol 16. 1864, pp 274, 504, 633-638, 770-774.

10.45. See 10.2. above; in series IR 27/1-323.

10.46. See 10.1 above; in series DC.1, DC.2 et seq.

10.47. See 10.2. above; in series 30/26/8 and /9.

10.48. All Souls College, Oxford OX1 4AL.

10.49. See 10.2. above; in series SP 12/109/39.

10.50. British Library, Newspaper Library, Colindale Avenue, London NW9 5HE.

Index

Post Script - The Church Assembly & General Synod

Although neither the Church Assembly nor the General Synod are ecclesiastical courts, a few words about each body are not inappropriate at the conclusion of this Cameo; both bodies were created in the twentieth century to aid the management of the Established Church and hence have contributed to the operation of church courts.

The *National Assembly of the Church of England* (the Assembly's correct title) was established in 1920, following an Enabling Act of Parliament of 1919 (The Church of England Assembly Powers Act), with authority to examine secular Statutes and promote Measures affecting the Church. The Assembly, unlike the Convocations (see Chapter 4), included worshipping laity, as well as clerics. The novel concept of involving lay persons in decisions - hitherto a clerical privilege - had been introduced by the Archbishops of Canterbury and York in the early 1890s; they had set up Houses of Laymen comprising individuals who had undergone Confirmation and who had been elected by Diocesan Conferences. In 1905 a *Representative Church Council* was constituted comprising the four Houses of the two Convocations and the two Houses of Laymen, but it had no statutory powers. When the Assembly was created in 1920 the qualification to be a lay representative was altered from a Confirmed Member to a Baptised Member of the Church of England. The Assembly, Chaired by the Archbishop of Canterbury, could (but did not always) meet three times a year.

A Measure, formally ratified by the Ecclesiastical Committee of Parliament and confirmed by Resolutions in the House of Commons and the House of Lords, in effect became Statute law. The Ecclesiastical Committee comprised 15 Lords and 15 Commoners nominated by, respectively, the Lord Chancellor and The Speaker. This Committee could not amend Measures but could refer them back to the Church Assembly if it believed a Measure to conflict with "the constitutional rights of the sovereign's subjects". Until 1919 only Parliament itself could change laws affecting the Church but in reality had found little time to do so for very many years.

The Church Assembly, similarly to its predecessor the Representative Church Council, had three Houses: Bishops, Clergy and Laity, and hence representation from the remotest small parish to the Primate of All England himself - but the Assembly had statutory powers. The House of Bishops consisted of the Upper Houses of the Convocations of Canterbury and York, while the House of Clergy comprised the Lower Houses of both Convocations. The House of Laity was composed of lay representatives from the Chamber of Laity, chosen from the Diocesan Conferences in each diocese in the country. The numbers of persons of the House of Laity were about the same as the total of the other two Houses. Between its creation in 1919 and 1941 the Assembly passed eighty Measures, in effect becoming Acts of Parliament, demonstrating the back-log of reform felt necessary early in the twentieth century.

The *General Synod of the Church of England*, with its own hierarchical structure, and presided over jointly by the Archbishops of Canterbury and York, replaced the Church Assembly in 1970 to offer greater democratic involvement of the laity, but performing very similar functions to those of the Assembly. The Houses of Bishops, Clergy and Laity were retained but in each parish in the country there is a parochial synod (the Parochial Church Council) feeding ideas nowadays through representation to a Deanery Synod and a Diocesan Synod (replacing the Diocesan Conference) to the House of Laity of the General Synod, which normally meets twice a year. When the Convocations are dissolved, in parallel with Parliament being dissolved, the General Synod is automatically dissolved, and the General Synod is reconvened when the new Convocations are called together. The two archbishops decide which of them shall take the Chair at a meeting of the General Synod. The relationship formerly enjoyed by the Assembly to the Ecclesiastical Committee and the constitution of that Committee have been maintained. Hence Measures and Canons today may originate in General Synod and its various advisory boards, commissions, committees and councils; but because of the structure described above they are, in effect, ratified by both Convocations before finally receiving the Royal Assent. A copy of the Constitution and Standing Orders of the General Synod are available from the General Synod or Church Information Office - see reference 10.25.

"The Act Books of Church courts are among the more strikingly repulsive of all the relics of the past - written in cramped and hurried hands, in very abbreviated and technical Latin, often preserved (if that is the right word) in fairly noisome conditions, ill-sorted and mostly unlisted, unindexed and sometimes broken into pieces. Cause papers, where they exist, are likely to be found in total confusion and with no guide to their contents. It is a great pity that the Church did not pay better attention to its records at a time when it had the money and leisure to do so; the heroic efforts of the present are handicapped by serious lack of both. Only young scholars, still enthusiastic, physically strong, and possessed of a sound digestion, are advised to tackle these materials. On the other hand, they offer a most promising field to research because they illuminate the history of Church and people in ways that no other source can. They take one to the realities. This is because of the wide range of cases that came before these courts, and because the range touched the human being so very near his personal centre."

G R Elton in *England 1200-1640*. Hodder and Stoughton. 1969.

The author of this Cameo believes that the situation in many archives has improved somewhat since Professor Elton wrote the above in 1969. Moreover, as explained elsewhere in this Cameo, most Ecclesiastical Court documents after 1733 appear in English and so become easier to follow. Even for the earlier records the quality of much of the Latin is quite poor; hence determined amateurs, whatever their ages or physical abilities, are likely to encounter fewer problems in reading the records than will many a Latin scholar from a purist academy.

* * *

It may be noted that many fascinating and unique aspects of probate records and associated indexes from the Provinces of Canterbury and York, with numerous references, were highlighted under the general heading of "The Probate Records of the Nation: New Approaches to Wills, Inventories and Accounts", a series of articles included in the British Record Society's *The Records of the Nation*, edited by G H Martin and Peter Spufford in 1988.